ENGLISH IN COMPUTING

ERIC H. GLENDINNING & JOHN McEWAN

UNWIN HYMAN

First published in 1987 by

UNWIN HYMAN LIMITED
15–17 Broadwick Street
London W1V 1FP

ISBN 7135 2799 4
Cassette 7135 2746 3

Edited by Stenton Associates
Designed by Ken Vail Graphic Design

Typset by Goodfellow & Egan, Cambridge

Printed and bound in Great Britain by Bell and Bain Ltd., Glasgow

Acknowledgements

The publishers are grateful to the following for permission to reproduce
copyright material. They have tried to contact all copyright holders but
where they have failed will be pleased to make the necessary arrangements
at the first opportunity.

Keyboard on page 22 taken from *BBC Microcomputer System User Guide*;
keyboard on page 30 courtesy of ACT (International) Limited; optical marks
example on page 41 courtesy of Data and Research Services Ltd.

Contents

Introduction

To the teacher

The book is organised into twelve units which cover the main areas of computer studies from systems to applications. Each unit is divided into five sections, each focussing on a different set of skills or language features:

Section One   Reading skills
Section Two   Language work
Section Three   Listening skills
Section Four   Terminology
Section Five   Writing skills

This text does not require a specialist knowledge of computers. But, like all English teaching, it requires an interest in meeting the language needs of your students. You will also find it useful to learn something about their subject. This book will provide a useful introduction for you.

These notes explain the objectives of each section and how to use the sections.

Section One
The reading text is divided into two parts. The first, and shorter part, introduces the theme and is used to develop prediction skills. Pre-reading tasks are set to give purpose to the students' reading. Students should be encouraged to guess the answers to these pre-questions and then check the text quickly for the correct answers. On this first quick reading they should try to ignore information which will not help them with the answers. Later units contain an information transfer exercise which requires a more detailed reading of the text.

The second part of the reading text contains most of the content. To divide the load, students are asked to work in pairs. Each pair member has a specific task to complete individually. The partners then combine their findings to solve problems together. This form of jigsaw reading develops the skill of reading for specific information and encourages listening and speaking, as the pairs should share their information orally. Teachers can set these reading and problem solving tasks as group, rather than pair, activities if they wish.

Some units contain Text Study exercises which provide help with features of cohesion and coherence. These features can act as useful guides to the reader when they are clearly understood.

Section Two
Key language items from the text are explained and practised. These items occur naturally and the texts have not been constructed to exemplify particular language features. The practice activities focus on use rather than form and are contextualised. In selected units the output from this section provides input for writing activities in Section Five.

Section Three
The listening section provides practice in dealing with the spoken language of description and explanation. Pre-listening tasks have been set to encourage prediction. The task format has also been used for the other listening activities,

rather than traditional comprehension questions, so that the students have a clear purpose. In selected units the output from these tasks is also used as input for writing activities in Section Five.

Students should attempt the pre-listening tasks individually. They may then compare answers. Next play the tape through without stopping. Students should then compare their answers in pairs or groups. Points of disagreement or gaps will provide focus for the second listening. This time the tape should be stopped at each of these points so that the students can decide on the correct answer. Finish by playing the tape through again without stopping.

Section Four
Understanding the English used in computing requires a knowledge of many new terms, including familiar words used in unfamiliar ways, eg dedicated. An understanding of these terms will come through reading and all key terms when first introduced are printed in **bold** type. These terms are also defined in the min-dictionary in Appendix 1. In addition, Section Four includes a set of vocabulary acquisition exercises to help the reader cope with the load. These include categorisation and using knowledge of word-formation. By checking their answers in Appendix 1, the students can also gain practice in basic reference skills.

Section Five
The writing section provides guided practice in writing brief texts. This serves two roles; it reinforces the language work covered in Section Two and provides practice in organising and presenting key types of writing including description, explanation, and comparison and contrast.

To the student

To get the most out of this book, you have to think. Use your brain, which is a more versatile instrument than a computer. Don't be a passive learner. With your partner, work out the solutions to the different activities. If you do not agree with the answer key, go back to the text and try again. Help in understanding technical terms may be obtained from the mini-dictionary in Appendix 1.

You can use this book on your own, although clearly you will not be able to practise your speaking skills! Follow the instructions for each task carefully. For pair activities, you will have to answer both parts. Use the answer key to check your answers. Remember that for some exercises, only examples are given. Your answer may be equally correct. If you are working without the cassette, treat the listening tasks as reading tasks and use the tapescripts as reading passages.

If you can combine study of this book with practical work with computers, you should gain even more from the text.

Thanks
The authors would like to thank the many overseas students at Edinburgh Language Foundation who have used these materials and helped give them their present shape.

UNIT ONE
Computer Systems

Section One Reading Skills

Task 1

Try to answer this question.

What type of computer is most suitable for home use?
1 mainframe **2** minicomputer **3** microcomputer

*When you have chosen your answer, read Text 1.1 quickly
to find out if you are right. Try to ignore information which
will not help you with the answer.*

TEXT 1.1

Computers can be divided into three main types, depending on their size and power.

Mainframe computers are the largest and most powerful. They can handle large amounts of information very quickly and can be used by many people at the same time. They usually fill a whole room and are sometimes referred to as **mainframes** or **computer installations**. They are found in large institutions like universities and government departments.

Minicomputers, commonly known as **minis**, are smaller and less powerful than mainframes. They are about the size of an office desk and are usually found in banks and offices. They are becoming less popular as microcomputers improve.

Microcomputers, commonly known as **micros**, are the smallest and least powerful. They are about the size of a typewriter. They can handle smaller amounts of information at a time and are slower than the other two types. They are ideal for use as home computers and are also used in education and business. More powerful microcomputers are gradually being produced, therefore they are becoming the most commonly used type of computers.

Task 2

Complete Table 1.1 using information from the text.

TABLE 1.1

	Mainframe	Minicomputer	Microcomputer
size		desk	
power	+++		
use			at home, in education and business

Task 3

Work in pairs, A and B. If working alone, do both parts.

Student A

Read Text 1.2 to find out what a **program** *is and what the functions are of these items:*
1 main memory
2 input device
3 storage device
Read only those parts of the text which will help you.

Student B

Read Text 1.2 to find out what **data** *is and what the functions are of these items:*
1 processor
2 output device
3 monitor
Read only those parts of the text which will help you.

Now explain your findings to your partner.

TEXT 1.2

A computer can do very little until it is given some information. This is known as the **input** and usually consists of a program and some data.   20

A **program** is a set of instructions, written in a special computer language, telling the computer what operations and processes have to be carried out and in what order they should be done. **Data,** however, is the particular information that has to be processed by the computer, e.g. numbers, names, measurements. Data brought out of the computer is known as the **output**.   25

EXAMPLE: A computer calculating 3 + 4 = 7 uses the following program and data:

PROGRAM   Add two numbers then display the result.   30
INPUT DATA   3,4
OUTPUT DATA   7

When a program is **run**, i.e. put into operation, the computer **executes** the program step by step to **process** the data. The same program can be used with different sets of data.   35

Information in the form of programs and data is called **software**, but the pieces of equipment making up the computer system are known as **hardware**.

The most important item of hardware is the **CPU** (Central Processing Unit). This is the electronic unit at the centre of the computer system. It   40 contains the processor and the main memory.

The **processor** is the brain of the computer. It does all the processing and controls all the other devices in the computer system.

The **main memory** is the part of the computer where programs and data being used by the processor can be stored. However it only stores   45 information while the computer is switched on and it has a limited capacity.

All the other devices in the computer system which can be connected to the CPU are known as **peripherals**. These include input devices, output devices and storage devices.   50

An **input device** is a peripheral which enables information to be fed into the computer. The most commonly used input device is a **keyboard**, similar to a typewriter keyboard.

An **output device** is a peripheral which enables information to be brought out of the computer, usually to display the processed data. The   55 most commonly used output device is a specially adapted television known as a **monitor** or **VDU** (Visual Display Unit). Another common output device is a **printer**. This prints the output of the CPU onto paper.

A **storage device** is a peripheral used for the permanent storage of information. It has a much greater capacity than the main memory and   60 commonly uses **magnetic tape** or **magnetic discs** as the **storage medium**.

These are the main pieces of hardware of any computer system whether a small 'micro' or a large mainframe system.

Task 4

*Work in pairs. Combine your findings from Task 3 to solve
these problems together.*

PROBLEM 1

Match each component in Column A with its function from Column B.

A *COMPONENT*

1 Storage device
2 Input device
3 Output device
4 Main memory
5 Processor

B *FUNCTION*

a It displays the processed data.
b It holds the programs and data
being used by the processor.
c It does all the processing and
controls the peripherals.
d It allows data to be entered.
e It provides permanent storage for
programs and data.

PROBLEM 2

Label this diagram of a computer system using these terms:

a main memory
d input device

b output device
e processor

c storage device

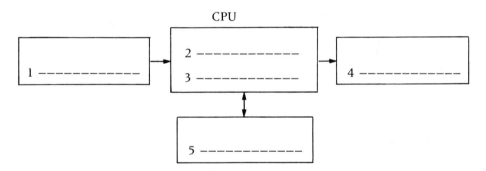

CPU

1 _____

2 _____

3 _____

4 _____

5 _____

Task 5

TEXT STUDY   Links between sentences: noun/pronoun

*Look again at Text 1.2 lines 39 to 41 and note how the writer
links parts of the text together using pronouns.*

The most important item of hardware is the CPU (Central Processing Unit). This
is the electronic unit at the centre of the computer system. It contains the
processor and the main memory.

*Try to find the links for each of these words.
Write down the word and line number:*

1	it (line 20)	**5**	it (line 46)
2	This (line 20)	**6**	These (line 49)
3	they (line 24)	**7**	This (line 58)
4	It (line 42)	**8**	It (line 60)

Section Two   Language Study

Study this data about minicomputers and microcomputers.

	Minicomputer	Microcomputer
size	desk	typewriter
power	++	+
use	in banks and offices	at home, in education and business

We can compare the two types like this:

SIZE   **1**   The minicomputer is bigger (than the micro).
        2   The microcomputer is smaller.
POWER   **3**   The minicomputer is more powerful (than the micro).
        4   The microcomputer is less powerful.
USE   **5**   Both minicomputers and microcomputers are used in business.

We can contrast the two types like this:

USE   **6**   The minicomputer is used in banks and offices but the micro is used at home, in education and in business.

Task 6

Go back to Table 1.1 in Task 2.
Write five sentences comparing and contrasting the
mainframe with the minicomputer.

Task 7

Look again at Table 1.1.
We can compare the three types of computers like this:

SIZE   **7**   The microcomputer is the smallest.
         8   The mainframe is the biggest.
POWER   **9**   The microcomputer is the least powerful.
        10   The mainframe is the most powerful.

Using the extra data below, complete these pairs of sentences:

	Mainframe	*Minicomputer*	*Microcomputer*
memory	+++	++	+
cost	+++	++	+

11   The mainframe has the biggest memory.

12   The microcomputer ....

13   The microcomputer is the least expensive.

14   The mainframe ....

15   The minicomputer ....

16   The microcomputer has a smaller memory than the minicomputer.

17   The minicomputer is more expensive than the microcomputer.

18   The microcomputer ....

Section Three   Listening Skills

Task 8

The way that a computer system is connected
together is known as the **system configuration**.

*Try to label these diagrams of computer system
configurations with these labels:*

a network   **b** stand-alone   **c** multi-user

Now listen to the tape to check your answers.

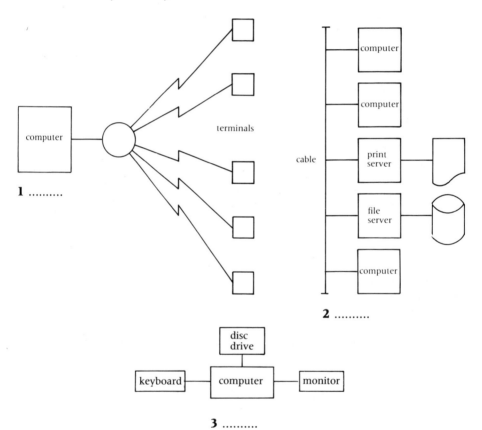

Section Four Terminology

Task 9

Often more than one term is used for the same component. Sometimes we can work out the meaning of these new terms by relating them to terms we already know.

Try to link each of the terms in column A with one of the terms in column B. The first one is done for you.

COLUMN A
1 main store
2 central processor
3 backing store
4 primary store
5 secondary store
6 monitor
7 internal memory
8 external memory
9 screen

COLUMN B
a CPU
b main memory
c VDU
d storage device

Check your answers in Appendix 1.

Section Five Writing Skills

Task 10

Look back at Table 1.1. Using the completed table, together with some of your answers from Tasks 6 and 7, complete the gaps in this text:

We can divide computers into three types: mainframe, minicomputer and microcomputer.

The mainframe is the biggest and most powerful. It is the size of.......................... .... and has the .... It is used in ....

The minicomputer is .... than a mainframe but is .... than a microcomputer. It is the size of .... and is used in ....

The microcomputer is the .... It is the size of .... It is the least .... and is used ....

UNIT TWO
Computer Access

Section One **Reading Skills**

Task 1

Try to answer these questions.

1 What is a cursor?
2 How can computer access be limited to certain people only?

When you have decided on answers, read Text 2.1 quickly to find out if you are right.

TEXT 2.1

When a microcomputer is switched on, a **signing-on message** appears
on the monitor screen. This gives information about the computer system
e.g. the make of computer, the amount of usable memory, the name of
the computer language in use.

A prompt and a cursor will also be displayed. The **prompt** consists of   5
one or more words or symbols e.g. READY, OK, ?, >. It indicates that the
computer is ready to accept input from the keyboard. The **cursor** usually
takes the form of a square or a flashing line i.e. ■ or ＼╵╱ . It indicates
where the next input will be displayed. As each input appears on the
screen, the cursor moves to a new position.   10

Although the input from the keyboard is displayed on the screen and
can be **edited** i.e. checked and corrected, it is not processed or stored in
the main memory until the RETURN key is pressed. The RETURN key
therefore has to be pressed at the end of each input.

If the use of the computer system, or part of it, is limited to certain people,   15
a secret **password** may have to be input. The password is not normally
displayed on the screen when it is keyed in. This prevents unauthorised
people from reading it.

If more than one language is available on the computer, the name of
the required language has to be input. The computer will respond with a   20
prompt and then only accept input in the chosen language. The language
BASIC is found on most microcomputers.

Task 2

Work in pairs, A and B. If working alone, do both parts.

Student A
Read Text 2.2 to find out how to **log in**
a mainframe terminal. Read only those
parts of the text which will help you.

Student B
Read Text 2.2 to find out how to **log out**
a mainframe terminal. Read only those
parts of the text which will help you.

Now explain your findings to your partner.

TEXT 2.2

Accessing a network or a multi-user system is slightly more complex. In this case, a **logging procedure** must be followed. This allows the computer to keep a **log** (or record) of when the terminal enters and leaves the system and how long it uses the CPU. The use of a mainframe CPU for processing is very expensive and the log provides a means of calculating the cost. Most of the time, however, is spent inputting and outputting data and this is not so expensive.

To enter the system the terminal must be **logged in**. A typical logging in procedure is as follows:
1 Switch on the terminal.
   An arrow prompt will appear on the screen.
2 Type LOGIN and press `RETURN`.
   The computer will display a prompt asking for an identification number.
3 Input your identification number.
   A prompt will now be displayed asking for a password.
4 Input the correct password.
   If the correct combination of identification number and password has been input, the computer will display a prompt indicating that the terminal now has access to the system.
5 Key in the name of the required language and press `RETURN` .
   A prompt will be displayed giving the name and version number of the chosen language.

When the user has finished using a terminal it must be **logged out**. A typical logging out procedure is as follows:
1 Input a command to bring you out of the language you are using e.g. QUIT will bring you out of the language BASIC.
   The computer will respond with a prompt e.g. ER!
2 Type LOGOUT and press `RETURN`.
   A prompt will be displayed on the screen indicating that the terminal no longer has access to the system. It will also give the date and time of logging out and the amount of time the CPU has been used.
3 Switch off the terminal.

Logging out frees the terminal for other people to use and prevents them from accessing your programs and data. The cost of using the CPU is charged to you until your terminal is logged out. However, after a fixed time delay, the computer will usually log out an unused terminal automatically.

60

Task 3

Now combine your findings to solve this problem.

Study Table 2.1 which shows the prompts displayed on the VDU screen and the action which should follow each prompt. Complete the table by entering the correct action from this list.

1 Input the correct password.
2 Switch off the terminal.
3 Input your identification number (e.g. 243726).
4 Type LOGOUT and press RETURN.
5 Type LOGIN and press RETURN.
6 Select a language.

TABLE 2.1

Prompt	Action
>	
User Id?	
Password?	
Terminal (23) logged in at 09'21 on 24 03 86 OK,	

ER!	
Terminal (23) logged out at 10'51 on 24 03 86. Time used: 1hr 30min terminal time, 2min 23sec CPU time, 3min 53 sec I/O time. User number: 243726	

Task 4

TEXT STUDY   Links between new and old information: *a/the*

Look again at lines 5 to 8 and note the links.

A prompt and a cursor will also be displayed. The **prompt** consists of one or more words or symbols e.g. READY, OK, ?, > . It indicates that the computer is ready to accept input from the keyboard. The **cursor** usually takes the form of a square or a flashing line i.e. ■ or ⊻ .

We often use 'a' or 'an' to show that a noun is new in a text. We use 'the' when the noun is used again, later in the text.

Find where each of these nouns are used later in the text. Write down the line number.

1 a microcomputer (line 1)
2 a secret **password** (line 16)
3 a multi-user system (line 23)
4 a **log** (line 25)
5 a password (line 38)

Section Two **Language Study**

Study these instructions for logging in and out of a computer system.

1 Switch on the terminal.
2 Type LOGIN and press RETURN.
3 Input your identification number.
4 Input the correct password.
5 Select a language.
6 Type QUIT and press RETURN.
7 Type LOGOUT and press RETURN.
8 Switch off the terminal.

We can change each instruction to make a description like this:

INSTRUCTION: Switch on the terminal.
DESCRIPTION: The terminal is switched on.

Task 5

Change the other instructions given above into descriptions. Be careful with the irregular verb 'input'. Its form does not change.

Section Three **Listening Skills**

Task 6

Study this list of BASIC commands. Try to guess what these commands are used for:

    SAVE
    LOAD
    RUN
    LIST

Task 7

Now listen to the tape. Write the name of each command in the correct space in this table.

Command	Action
1	Copies a program from a storage medium to the main memory.
2	Lists a program, line by line, on the VDU screen.
3	Starts the execution of the program in the main memory.
4	Copies a program from the main memory to a storage medium.

Section Four **Terminology**

Task 8

Initials (the first letters of words) and abbreviations (short forms of words) are often used in computing.

You should know the meaning of these examples from this and earlier units. Write down their meaning.

1 CPU
2 VDU
3 PC
4 mini
5 micro
6 Id.

Check your answers using Appendix 1.

Task 9

Use Appendix 1 to find out the meaning of the following initials and abbreviations.

1 OCR
2 ASCII
3 LAN
4 NLQ
5 CAD

Section Five **Writing Skills**

Task 10

Study these descriptions from Task 5. Each describes an action when logging in.

1 The terminal is switched on.
2 LOGIN is typed and `RETURN` is pressed.
3 Your identification number is input.
4 The correct password is input.
5 A language is selected.

Now study these sentences. They describe the effects which follow from each action. Match each action (1 to 5) with the correct effect (a to e).

a A prompt is displayed asking for a password.
b The computer indicates that the terminal has access to the system.
c An arrow prompt appears on the screen.
d The computer accepts input in that language.
e The computer displays a prompt asking for an Id. number.

Task 11

We can link an action and its result using **when**.
For example,

When the terminal is switched on, an arrow prompt appears on the screen.

Note the comma (,) between each action and its result.

We can put actions in sequence using these words:

First   then   after that   next   finally.

For example,

> First the terminal is switched on. Then LOGIN is typed and
> RETURN is pressed.

Now complete the blanks in this paragraph.

LOGGING IN

Before using a mainframe computer terminal, the user must log in. First,

the terminal .... When it is switched

on, ... Next LOGIN is typed

.... When this is done, ...

Then your identification number is input. When this is input ....

.... After that, the correct password is

input. .... , the computer indicates that

the terminal has access to the system. Finally, a language is selected.

When this is done, ...

UNIT THREE
Computer Keyboards

Section One **Reading Skills**

Task 1

*Read Text 3.1 quickly to find out the answers to these
questions. Try to ignore information which does not help
you with the answers.*

1 What is similar between a computer keyboard
   and a typewriter keyboard?
2 What is different between a computer
   keyboard and a typewriter keyboard?

TEXT 3.1

A **keyboard** is one of the most common input devices used with
computers. It allows the user to key in programs and data and to
control the computer system. The alphabetic and numeric keys are
arranged in the same order as a typewriter. This layout is known as
QWERTY because these are the first six letters on the top left of the   5
keyboard.

Letters, numbers, symbols and blank spaces are known as **characters**.
Computer keyboards have all the characters found on typewriters. In
addition, they have some extra characters and some keys that do not
produce characters but have special uses.   10

As with electric typewriters, most keys are **auto-repeating**. This means
that, if they are held down, they repeat the same function again and again
until they are released.

Unlike a typewriter, when using a computer keyboard, it is particularly
important not to confuse the number 0 key with the letter O key and the   15
number 1 with the letter l.

Task 2

Study this diagram of a typical computer keyboard. Write down the names of the keys which are not found on typewriter keyboards. Compare your answers with your neighbour.

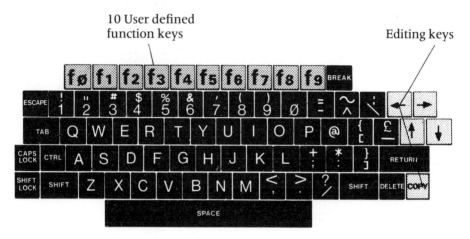

Task 3

Read Text 3.2 to find out the function of these keys:

1 **SHIFT**   2 **SHIFT LOCK**   3 **CAPS LOCK**

Write their function in Table 3.1.

TABLE 3.1

Key	Function
SHIFT	
SHIFT LOCK	
CAPS LOCK	

TEXT 3.2

Most character keys can produce two different characters depending on whether or not the **SHIFT**, **SHIFT LOCK** or **CAPS LOCK** functions are in operation.

EXAMPLE: The **A** key can produce the upper-case character A or the   20
lower-case character a.

The **&/6** key can produce the upper-case character & or
the lower-case character 6.

If a character key is pressed without using the **SHIFT** **SHIFT LOCK** or
CAPS LOCK functions, the lower-case character is produced.   25

EXAMPLE: If **SHIFT**, **SHIFT LOCK** and **CAPS LOCK** are not used,

the **A** key produces the character a and
the **&/6** key produces the character 6.

If **SHIFT** is held down while a character key is pressed, the upper-case
character is produced.   30

EXAMPLE: If **SHIFT** is held down,

the **A** key produces the upper-case character A and

the **&/6** key produces the upper-case character & .

The **SHIFT LOCK** function keeps the **SHIFT** in operation without having
to hold down the **SHIFT** key. It is switched on by the **SHIFT LOCK**   35
key. This is used when only upper-case characters are required.
The **SHIFT LOCK** function can be switched off again by pressing the
SHIFT LOCK key a second time.

The **CAPS LOCK** function is similar to the **SHIFT LOCK** function.
However, the **CAPS LOCK** function produces a mixture of upper-case   40
and lower-case characters. It is switched on by pressing the **CAPS LOCK**
key once. The alphabetic keys will then produce capital letters but all the
other character keys will produce lower-case characters.

EXAMPLE: If **CAPS LOCK** is on,

the **A** key produces the upper-case character A and   45

the **&/6** key produces the lower-case character 6.

The combination of capital letters and numbers produced is particularly
useful when using computer languages. The **CAPS LOCK** function, therefore, is normally in operation when the computer is first switched on.

Task 4

Now complete Table 3.2 to show what happens when different keys are pressed with and without `SHIFT`, `SHIFT LOCK` *and* `CAPS LOCK`.

TABLE 3.2

Key	Without `SHIFT` `SHIFT LOCK` *or* `CAPS LOCK`	With `SHIFT` *or* `SHIFT LOCK`	With `CAPS LOCK`
1 A	a	A	A
2 &6	6	&	
3 =			
4 I			
5 +;			
6 B			
7 ?/			
8 O			
9 Ø			
10 !1			

Task 5

Work in pairs, A and B. If working alone, do both parts.

Student A

Find the position of these keys on the keyboard shown in Task 2. Then read Text 3.3 to find out their functions.
1 `BREAK`
2 `SPACE`
3 `←` `→` `↑` `↓`
Write their functions briefly in Table 3.3.

Student B

Find the position of these keys on the keyboard shown in Task 2. Then read Text 3.3 to find out their functions.
1 `RETURN`
2 `ESCAPE`
3 `COPY`
Write their functions briefly in Table 3.3.

TABLE 3.3

Key	Function
SPACE	
RETURN	
DELETE	Removes the character on the left of the cursor from the VDU screen.
ESCAPE	
BREAK	
CTRL (control)	Switches various functions on and off if held down while another key is pressed. EXAMPLE: CTRL held down while the B key is pressed switches the printer on.
TAB	Moves the cursor one space to the right but can be programmed to move the cursor any fixed number of spaces to the right (tabulations).
COPY	
User-defined function keys	Do not operate until they are programmed by the user. Can be programmed to produce any characters or to perform various functions.
Cursor keys (Arrow keys)	

TEXT 3.3

The long key at the bottom of the keyboard is known as the **SPACE** bar.   50
It produces a blank space each time it is pressed. However, this space is
considered to be a character and uses as much of the main memory as any
other character.

The **RETURN** (or ENTER) key is particularly important and is used
frequently. The characters displayed on the monitor screen are not   55
processed or entered into the main memory until the **RETURN** key is
pressed. The **RETURN** key must therefore be pressed to complete each
input and begin a new line.

The key allows the user to stop a program at any time without
losing the data or the program from the main memory.   60

The BREAK key provides a means of resetting the computer to its
original condition. It clears the program and all the data from the main
memory. Therefore, it should not normally be used to stop a program.

The **cursor** keys, also known as **arrow** keys, move the cursor to
any position on the VDU screen in the direction of the arrows.   65

The COPY key allows characters to be copied from one part of the VDU
screen to another without having to press the individual character keys.

The COPY key and the **cursor** keys are together known as **editing**
keys because they allow the user to edit programs and data on the VDU
screen quickly and easily.   70

Task 6

*Now complete Table 3.3 by exchanging information orally
with your partner.*

*When you have completed the exchange, look at each
other's tables to check you have copied correctly.*

*The table contains information about other important keys
not described in the text. Find the position of these keys on
the keyboard and make sure you understand their
function.*

Task 7

Study this computer program. Compare it with the screen display.

Each line in the display has mistakes resulting from one keyboard error. For example, one wrong key has been pressed or held down.

Working with your partner, try to decide what caused the mistake on each line of the screen display.

PROGRAM
50 **PRINT** "Temperature in degrees Fahrenheit:"
60 **INPUT F**
70 **LET C** = (F–32)*5/9
80 **PRINT**
90 **PRINT F;** "degrees Fahrenheit = ";C;" degrees Celsius"
100 **PRINT**
110 **END**

SCREEN DISPLAY

```
   50  PRINT 2Temperature in degrees fahrenheit: 2
   60  INPUTF
   70  LET C = (F–32)*5?9
   80  PRINTTTTTTTT
   )0  PRINT F+" DEGREES FAHRENHEIT = "+C+" DEGREES CELSIUS"
 1OO  PRINT
  110  end
```

Task 8

TEXT STUDY   *because   therefore   however*

Meaning links are words used in texts to link ideas together. They help us to understand the way the writer has connected important parts of the text. Here are some common meaning links and the ideas they join.

Because   links a statement and a reason. It answers the question 'Why?' For example,

Computer and typewriter keyboards are similar **because** both have a QWERTY layout.

Therefore links a statement and a result. It answers
the question 'What is the result of this?'
For example,

The **BREAK** key clears the program and
all the data from the main memory,
therefore it should be used with care.

Note the comma (,) before **therefore.**

However links a statement and a qualification. It
means 'There is something extra or
unexpected coming'. For example,

When you type a line of characters, they
appear on the screen. **However,** they are
not processed or entered into the main
memory until the **RETURN** key is pressed.

Note that **However** is separated from the rest of
the sentence by a comma.

Read through this text. It contains four blanks. Insert
because, therefore *or* **however** *in each blank,*
whichever is correct.

A computer keyboard is similar to a typewriter keyboard .... 1 ....
it has alphabetic and numeric keys in a QWERTY layout. .... 2 .... ,
there are some differences. For example, the computer keyboard has
user-defined function keys. Their use depends on how they are
programmed, ... 3 .... it varies from program to program.
Some computer keyboards have a **BREAK** key. It must be used with
care .... 4 .... it clears the program and all the data from the
main memory.

Section Two **Language Study**

Study these two actions:

1 The `CAPS LOCK` is pressed.
2 The letter keys produce capital letters.

Action 2 follows directly from action 1. As you learned in Unit Two, we can link them using the time word **when.**

> **When** the `CAPS LOCK` is pressed, the letter keys produce capital letters.

Task 9

Look at Table 3.2 in Task 4. Write five sentences like this,

> When A is pressed without `SHIFT` `SHIFT LOCK` or `CAPS LOCK` a is produced.

Now study these two actions:

3 The `SHIFT LOCK` gives capital letters and upper-case symbols.
4 You press it again.

Action 4 marks the limit of action 3. It tells us when action 3 ends. We can link both actions using the time word **until.**

> The `SHIFT LOCK` gives capital letters and upper-case symbols **until** you press it again.

We do not use a comma when a time word comes in the middle of a sentence.

Task 10

*Match each action from column A with its limit from
column B. Then link the two using* **until.**

A	B
1 With ⬛ the letter keys produce capital letters	**a** ⬛ is released
2 When you hold down ⬛ the number keys produce upper-case characters	**b** the key is released
3 An input is not processed or entered into the main memory	**c** the ⬛ is released
4 The function keys do not operate	**d** ⬛ is released
5 When you hold down a key, the keyboard repeats the same function again and again	**e** ⬛ is pressed
6 When you press ⬛ the ⬛ function stays in operation	**f** they are programmed by the user

Section Three **Listening Skills**

Task 11

*Try to identify some of the differences between this
keyboard and the keyboard shown in Section One.
Note them in Table 3.4.*

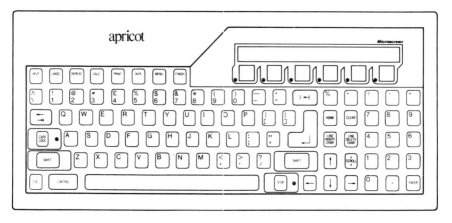

TABLE 3.4

Extra keys	Missing keys	Different labels	Different keyboard positions

Task 12

Listen to the tape to check if your answers are correct.
Then note any additional differences described.

Section Four **Terminology**

Task 13

Study Table 3.5 which lists the names of the symbols
found on a computer keyboard. Find their positions on
the keyboard shown in Section One.

Task 14

Study this line of a program,

$$60 \text{ IF S}=7 \text{ THEN PRINT "YES"}$$

This would be read as,

Sixty space if space S equals seven space then space
print space open quotes yes (in capitals) close quotes

Use Table 3.5 to read out these computer program lines.

1 30 IF S$ = "END" THEN GOTO 200
2 25 LET T = T + (F*2/N)
3 40 PROC_move:INPUT "Cost of 100 @ 10P ? "; C
4 20 IF M% > −1 OR M% < 12 THEN PRINT "Can't use"
5 60 LDA &10\MASK :.LOOP BIT VIA +13

TABLE 3.5

!	exclamation mark (pling, shriek)
"	quotes (quotation marks, inverted commas)
#	hash
$	dollar (string)
%	percent
&	ampersand
'	apostrophe
(	open bracket (left bracket)
)	close bracket (right bracket)
=	equals (becomes)
−	hyphen (dash, minus)
@	at sign
+	plus
;	semicolon
*	star (asterisk)
:	colon (ellipsis)
<	less than
,	comma
>	greater than
.	stop (dot, period, full stop, point)
?	question mark (query)
/	oblique (solidus, slash)
~	tilde
^	caret (hat)
|	vertical bar (double bar)
\	backslash
{	open brace (left brace)
[	open square bracket (left square bracket)
£	pound sign
_	underscore (underline)
}	close brace (right brace)
]	close square bracket (right square bracket)

TABLE 3.6

When doing mathematics, the following symbols are used:

+	plus
−	minus
*	multiplied by (times)
/	divided by
^	raised to the power of
=	equals
<>	not equal to
<	less than
>	greater than
<=	less than or equal to
>=	greater than or equal to

Task 15

Work in pairs, A and B.

Student A
*Read out Program 1 for your partner
to write down.*

Student B
*Read out Program 2 for your partner
to write down.*

When you have finished, compare your answers with the original programs.

PROGRAM 1

```
10  CLS
20  PRINT "Do you want to leave this program (Y/N)?";
30  answer$ = GET$
40  IF answer$ <> "Y" AND answer$ <> "N" GOTO 30
50  IF answer$ = "N" GOTO 20
60  PRINT' "Goodbye!": END
```

PROGRAM 2

```
10  CLS
20  INPUT' "Input a number (1–10)." number%
30  PRINT' "Your number was "; number%
40  IF number% > 10 PRINT' "TOO BIG!": GOTO 20
50  IF number% < = 0 PRINT' "Try a number > 0.":GOTO 20
60  END
```

Section Five **Writing Skills**

Study these pieces of information:

1 They are similar to typewriter keyboards.
2 Typewriter keyboards have the same QWERTY layout.

We can combine information about the same topic like this:

1+2 They are similar to typewriter keyboards **which** have the same
QWERTY layout.

Task 16

Now combine each of these sets of information in the same way:

3 The computer keyboard has extra keys.
4 The extra keys have special functions.

5 There are editing keys.
6 The editing keys allow the user to edit data
   on the VDU screen.

7 There are user-defined function keys.
8 The user-defined function keys can be
   programmed to suit the user.

9 The **RETURN** key has an extra function.
10 This function is not usually required on
   typewriters.

*Now complete this summary of this Unit by entering your
sentences in the correct place.*

Keyboards are the most commonly used input devices. **1 + 2**. However, there
are some important differences. **3 + 4**. For example, **5 + 6**. In addition, **7 + 8**.
9 + 10. It causes the characters on the screen to be processed or stored in the
main memory.

UNIT FOUR
Input Devices

Section One **Reading Skills**

Task 1

Try to answer these questions.

1 What is the difference between a device being
   online and a device being **offline**?
2 What is a **key station**?

*Now read Text 4.1 quickly to check your answers or to find the right answers. Try
to ignore information which does not help you.*

TEXT 4.1

Inputting large amounts of data using a keyboard may take up a lot of
computer time if the keyboard is **online** i.e. connected to and controlled
by the CPU. For this reason, data is often prepared on an **offline**
keyboard device i.e. one which is not connected to or controlled by the
computer.   5

In the past, a **keypunch** was used with mainframe computer systems. This
device caused the input from a keyboard to be punched, as a series of
holes, onto pieces of thin cardboard called **punched cards** (see Fig. 4.1).

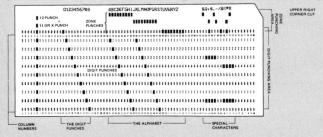

FIG. 4.1
The punched cards were later fed through an online input device called a
card reader which read the data from the holes and transferred it to the   10
main memory of the computer.

However, punched cards have been replaced by much faster **key-to-disc**
and **key-to-tape systems.** These use offline **key stations** which transfer data, keyed in on a keyboard, to magnetic discs or magnetic tape. The
data can later be transferred from the discs or tape to the main memory   15
of the computer at high speed. Magnetic media such as discs or tape
provide a much more compact means of storing data than punchcards.

Task 2

Work in pairs, A and B. If working alone, do both parts.

Student A

Read these sections of Text 4.2 and try to match each input device described with one of the illustrations in Fig 4.2.

1 keypads and touchpads
2 other input devices

Student B

Read these sections of Text 4.2 and try to match each input device described with one of the illustrations in Fig 4.2.

1 cursor control devices
2 drawing devices

TEXT 4.2

Although the keyboard is the most commonly used input device, many other more specialised input devices can be connected to the computer. However, most of them can only be used with programs specially written to suit them.   20

These specialised input devices can be divided into different types as follows:

Keypads and touchpads

A **numeric keypad** is a small keyboard with keys arranged like a calculator, allowing a lot of numerical data and calculations to be input   25 easily. On some computers the keypad is part of the main keyboard, to the right of the alphanumeric keys.

A **touchpad** has pictures or symbols which only have to be touched to input information. This is particularly useful for people who find the keyboard difficult to use e.g. young children. It is also useful in situations   30 where only simple input is required.

Cursor control devices

Some input devices are used to move the cursor around the screen. These include mice, trackerballs and joysticks.

A **mouse** is a small box with a ball underneath. When it is rolled in any direction across the surface of a desk, the cursor moves across the VDU   35 screen in the same direction. In this way the mouse can be used to point the cursor at special symbols on the screen. These special symbols are known as **icons**. They represent the processes that can be carried out by the program. By pointing the cursor at the required icon and pressing a button on the mouse, the process is put into operation. Mice and icon   40 programs are often used by businessmen, allowing them to control the computer easily while sitting at an office desk.

A **trackerball** is similar to a mouse but this device has the ball on top. To move the cursor on the screen, the user rotates the ball using his fingers.

To operate a **joystick**, the user grips and moves a vertical lever. The   45
movement of the lever causes the cursor to move around the screen.
Pressing a button on the joystick puts the required process into operation.
Cursor movements can be made very quickly using this device, therefore
it is often used for playing fast action games.

Drawing devices

Input devices used for **CAD** (Computer-Aided Design) include lightpens   50
and graphics tablets.

A **lightpen** is similar in shape to an ordinary pen. It is held against the
VDU screen and works by sending signals to the computer when it senses
the light given off by the screen. This enables the computer to calculate
the lightpen's position. As it is moved, lines are displayed on the screen.   55
The special program used with the lightpen allows the lines to be
increased or decreased in size or moved to different positions. In this way,
it can be used to 'draw' directly on the screen.

A **graphics tablet** has a flat board (or tablet) across which a pen is
moved. By using the reflection of light, ultrasound, or other methods, the   60
graphics tablet can measure the distance of the pen from the sides of the
tablet and therefore calculate its position. As the pen is moved across the
tablet, lines are displayed on the monitor screen. Detailed drawings can
be copied by placing them on the tablet and tracing over them with
the pen.   65

Other input devices

A **voice recognition device** allows the user to input data by speaking
into a microphone. The computer compares the input with the sound
patterns of words stored in the memory. To reduce the amount of
memory required, the vocabulary used with these devices is limited to a
few words. However, the large amount of memory needed to analyse the   70
input makes it difficult to use these devices with small microcomputers.

Measuring devices connected to a computer allow scientists to
monitor processes by making frequent measurements and analysing the
results. The measurements are usually of **analogue signals** i.e. signals
which vary in continuous manner. Before they are fed into the computer,   75
they must be changed into **digital signals** i.e. into pulses of electricity
which vary in steps. This is done by a component known as an **ADC**
(Analogue to Digital Converter).

FIG. 4.2

Task 3

*Now complete Table 4.1 together. Write the picture
number for each device in column B.*

TABLE 4.1

A device	B picture
keypunch	
numeric keypad	
touchpad	
mouse	
trackerball	
joystick	
lightpen	
graphics tablet	
voice recognition device	
measuring device	

Task 4

Solve these problems in pairs.

What kind of input device would best suit each of these requirements?

1 To input mathematical information.
2 To copy engineering drawings.
3 To guide a rocket in a computer game.
4 To help a busy manager to find a file quickly.
5 To help disabled people who cannot move their arms and legs.
6 To design new components without first making a large number of drawings.
7 To help young children learn to spell.

Section Two **Language Study**

Task 5

Find the answers to these questions in Text 4.2.

1 How is a mouse used to select a process?
2 How does a graphics tablet calculate the position of the pen on the tablet?
3 How can drawings be copied with a graphics tablet?

The easiest way to answer a **how** question like these is to use **by + −ing**. We can use this form to give information on the way things work. For example,

> Drawings can be copied with a graphics tablet **by** placing them on the tablet and tracing over them with a pen.

Task 6

Complete these sentences using the information in Text 4.1 and Text 4.2.

1 A mouse is used to select a process by ....
2 A graphics tablet calculates the position of the pen by ....
....
3 You can input information with a touchpad by ....
....
4 With a trackerball the cursor is moved on the screen by ....
....
5 A card reader gets information from a punched card by ....
....
6 Using a lightpen, lines can be 'drawn' on the screen by ....
....

There are two other ways we use to describe how things work.

Study this information about a trackerball.

1 The ball is rotated.
2 The cursor moves on the screen.

1 is a cause and 2 is an effect.

We can link a cause and an effect using **cause** + **to**-verb. For example,

> The ball is rotated. This **causes** the cursor **to** move on the screen.

Sometimes we can join the two actions into one sentence. For example,

> The ball is rotated, **which causes** the cursor **to** move on the screen.
> The ball is rotated, **causing** the cursor **to** move on the screen.

Study this information about a mouse.

1 The mouse has a ball underneath.
2 The mouse can be rolled across an office desk.

1 permits or allows 2 to happen. We can link these two facts using
allow + **to**-verb. For example,

> The mouse has a ball underneath. This **allows** it **to be** rolled across an
> office desk.

Sometimes we can join the two facts into one sentence. For example,
> The mouse has a ball underneath, **which allows** it **to be** rolled across an
> office desk.

> The mouse has a ball underneath, **allowing** it **to be** rolled across an
> office desk.

Task 7

*Study this information about different input devices. Link each set with either **cause** or*
allow, *whichever is correct. You may change or add words to the completed sentences.*

1 **Numeric keypad**	It has keys like a calculator. Numerical data can be input easily.
2 **Joystick**	The lever can be moved in any direction. The cursor moves quickly about the screen.
3 **Lightpen**	It is moved across the monitor screen. The user can 'draw' on the screen.
4 **Voice recognition devices**	They recognise simple spoken commands. Disabled people can use computers without touching controls.
5 **Keypunch**	The operator uses the keypunch. A series of holes are punched on cards.

Section Three **Listening Skills**

Task 8

The illustrations in Fig. 4.3 show four types of marks which can be read directly by computer input devices.

Try to label the illustrations using these terms:

1 Optical marks
2 Optical characters
3 Bar code
4 Magnetic ink characters

FIG. 4.3

a

9 780713 525861

b

ABCDEFGHIJKLM

NOPQRSTUVWXYZ

0123456789 . ¬

{ } % ? ♪ Ч Н : ; = + / $

c

d

Date of Birth		
Day	Month	Year
3 1	**July**	**4 6**
[0] [0]	Jan ⊏⊐	[0] [0]
[1] ◀▔▶	Feb ⊏⊐	[1] [1]
[2] [2]	Mar ⊏⊐	[2] [2]
◀▬ [3]	Apr ⊏⊐	[3] [3]
[4]	May ⊏⊐	◀▬ [4]
[5]	Jun ⊏⊐	[5] [5]
[6]	Jul ⊏▬	[6] ◀▬
[7]	Aug ⊏⊐	[7] [7]
[8]	Sep ⊏⊐	[8] [8]
[9]	Oct ⊏⊐	[9] [9]
	Nov ⊏⊐	
	Dec ⊏⊐	

Task 9

Now listen to the tape. Check your answers to Task 8.
Then match each of these methods to its application in
Table 4.2:

OMR (Optical Mark Recognition)
Bar codes
OCR (Optical Character Recognition)
MICR (Magnetic Ink Character Recognition)

TABLE 4.2

Method	*Application*
1	Read cheques for sorting codes and account numbers.
2	Read bills, passports, etc.
3	Identify items of food in a supermarket.
4	Mark exam papers quickly.

Section Four **Terminology**

Task 10

Complete Table 4.3 showing related terms. All of the
terms mentioned have been used earlier in the book.
TABLE 4.3

1	input device	output device
2	_____	hardware
3	alphabetic keys	_____
4	_____	lower-case characters
5	analogue signal	_____
6	program	_____
7	_____	secondary store
8	internal memory	_____
9	online	_____
10	_____	log out

Section Five **Writing Skills**

We can explain how a device works by using the different structures studied in this unit.

Study how a brief explanation can be made from these notes.

Voice recognition devices

1 Transform human speech signals into electrical signals.
2 Recognise simple spoken commands.
3 Disabled people can use computers without touching the controls.

Voice recognition devices work by transforming human speech signals into electrical signals. They recognise simple spoken commands. This allows disabled people to use computers without touching the controls.

Task 11

Try to write your own explanations from these notes.

Joystick

1 Transforms movements of the stick into movements on the VDU screen.
2 The stick can be moved in any direction.
3 The cursor can be moved quickly around the screen.

Trackerball

1 Transforms movements of the ball into movements of the cursor on the screen.
2 The cursor is pointed at the required icon on the screen.
3 The button is pressed.
4 The process is put into operation.

Task 12

Now write your own explanation of any other input device you know. Appendix 1 may help with details.

UNIT FIVE
Output Devices

Section One Reading Skills

Task 1

Try to answer these questions.

1 What does **monochrome** mean?
2 What is a **pixel?**
3 What is the difference between a **high resolution** and a **low resolution** display?

Now read Text 5.1 to check your answers.

TEXT 5.1

> The most commonly used output device is a **VDU** which has a screen for displaying information. This may be an ordinary television but a specially adapted television, known as a **monitor**, gives a much better quality display.
>
> **Monochrome monitors** can only display one colour. This is usually   5 either green or amber since these colours cause the user the least eyestrain. **Colour monitors**, on the other hand, are capable of displaying many colours.
>
> To produce the display, the computer sends signals to separate sections of the screen, causing dots of light to appear in each section. These screen   10 sections are called **pixels** (picture elements).
>
> If the computer divides the screen into a large number of small pixels, a very detailed, **high resolution** display is produced. This is suitable for displaying text and high quality graphics but uses up a lot of the computer's memory.   15
>
> On the other hand, if the computer divides the screen into a smaller number of large pixels, a less detailed, **low resolution** display is produced (see Fig. 5.1).
>
> FIG. 5.1      
>
>   high resolution   low resolution

This is adequate for text and crude graphics and uses up less of the computer's memory.

20

The resolution of the display can be changed by changing the **screen mode** of the computer.

Task 2

Work in pairs, A and B. If working alone, do both tasks.

Student A

Read Text 5.2 quickly to find out what kind of printer each of the following is:

1 daisywheel
2 ink-jet
3 line

Table 5.1 classifies printers. Write each of these printers in the correct section of the table.

Student B

Read Text 5.2 quickly to find out what kind of printer each of the following is:

1 dot-matrix
2 laser
3 thermal

Table 5.1 classifies printers. Write each of these printers in the correct section of the table.

Now exchange information with your partner, to complete your table.

TEXT 5.2

Another common output device is a **printer**. This gives a **hardcopy printout** i.e. the computer output is printed on paper.

There are many different types of printers. To decide which one is most suitable for a particular application, factors such as cost, speed, noise output and print quality have to be taken into consideration.

25

Impact printers print by forcing a print head into contact with an inked ribbon and paper.

One common type of impact printer is a **daisywheel printer**. This has solid characters positioned around a wheel (see Fig. 5.2).

30

FIG. 5.2

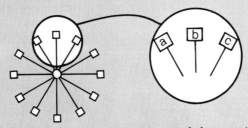

The wheel is rotated to the correct position and the required character is hammered against the ribbon and paper. This type of printer cannot print graphics and is very slow, having a maximum print rate of about 60 characters per second (60 cps). However the quality of print is very good. It produces what is referred to as Letter Quality (**LQ**) print. 35

Another common type of impact printer is a **dot-matrix printer**. This uses pins to print a pattern of dots in the shape of the required character (see Fig. 5.3).

FIG. 5.3

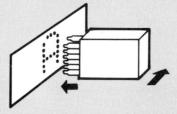

It can print text and graphics at rates up to about 200 cps. However, the quality of the print is not as good. The best print that can be achieved with this type of printer is known as Near Letter Quality (**NLQ**) print. 40

Although these types of printers are inexpensive, they can be quite noisy. **Non-impact printers**, on the other hand, give almost silent printing by using methods that do not require mechanical contact between the print head and the paper e.g. heat, electrostatics and lasers. 45

A **thermal printer** is an example of an inexpensive non-impact printer. It uses heated wires to print characters on special heat sensitive paper and can have a print rate of about 80 cps. However, having to use special paper adds to the running costs and is often inconvenient. 50

Another type of non-impact printer is an **ink-jet printer**. It operates by firing a fine spray of quick-drying ink at the paper. The ink jet is formed into the required character by electrostatic fields. This type of printer is quite fast and can print at rates of up to about 400 cps.

All the above types of printers are known as **character printers** because they only print one character at a time. They are also considered to be **slow printers** in computer terms. 55

Mainframe computers need printers that are very fast. These **fast printers** include line printers and laser printers.

Line printers may be impact or non-impact types. Impact line printers have solid characters on a moving chain or rotating drum but non-impact line printers use electrostatics to form the ink into the shapes of the characters. Line printers print a line of text at a time and can have print rates of about 3,000 lines per minute (3,000 lpm). However, they are very expensive. 60

65

Laser printers are extremely fast, printing a complete page at a time. They are non-impact printers which form an image on a light sensitive drum by scanning it with a laser beam. The image is then transferred to paper using special powdered ink. They can have a print rate of about 20,000 lpm but they are very expensive. 70

These are only a few of the many types of printers available. The techniques used by these printers are constantly being improved.

TABLE 5.1

	Impact	Non-impact
S l o w		
F a s t		

Task 3

Solve these problems in pairs. What kind of printer would best suit each of these requirements?

1 A small business which wants to produce letters directly from the computer of a quality good enough to send to customers.
2 An engineering firm who want rough copies of diagrams and text for use within the company.
3 A company who require quite a fast printer for their minicomputer which does not need special paper and which will not disturb the work of the office.
4 A major insurance company who need to produce large quantities of high quality text from their mainframe computer. They would prefer a silent device.
5 A mail-order company who want to produce large quantities of letters to their customers. They have a mainframe computer with a special print room and therefore don't have to worry about noise.

Section Two **Language Study**

Task 4

Table 5.2 below lists some of the input and output devices you have studied in this unit and the previous unit.

TABLE 5.2

Input device	Application
1 numeric keypad	input mathematical data
2 mouse	
3 lightpen	
4 joystick	
5 voice recognition device	
Output device	
6 high resolution monitor	
7 low resolution monitor	
8 daisywheel printer	
9 laser printer	
10 non-impact printer	

Add to the table the correct application for each device from this list.
Number 1 has been entered for you as an example.

a draw on the screen
b control computers by speech
c display high-quality graphics
d input mathematical data
e print 'letter quality' text
f play fast action games
g print text silently
h print text very quickly
i select a process easily from a menu
j display text and crude graphics

Task 5

We can link a device and its application in two ways. For example,

1 A numeric keyboard **is used to input** mathematical data.
2 A numeric keyboard **is used for inputting** mathematical data.

Describe the applications of each device listed in Table 5.2 in the same way.

Section Three **Listening Skills**

Task 6

What do you think are the applications of the forms of output listed in Table 5.3?

Write your answers in the table.

TABLE 5.3

Form of output	Application
1 Computer output on microfilm	
2 Machine control	
3 Voice output	

Task 7

Now listen to the tape. Check if your answers are correct.
Write in any extra information to improve your answer.

Section Four **Terminology**

Task 8

Many terms used in computing consist of two
nouns, for example, **lightpen.** The first noun
describes the second noun in a number of ways.

Study these examples.

1	lightpen	a pen **which is sensitive to** light
2	bar code	a code **which is made up of** printed bars
3	graphics tablet	a tablet **which is used for** drawing graphics
4	drum plotter	a plotter **which has** a drum

Try to define each of these terms in the same way. When
you have finished, check your answers in Appendix 1.

1	touchpad	6	impact printer
2	storage device	7	daisywheel printer
3	flatbed plotter	8	disc drive
4	laser printer	9	voice recognition device
5	colour monitor	10	line printer

Section Five **Writing Skills**

Study these facts about printers.

Impact	Non-impact
mechanical contact between print head and paper	no mechanical contact between print head and paper
noisy	silent
e.g. daisywheel	e.g. thermal

Note how we can classify printers.

> Printers **can be divided into** impact and non-impact printers.

Note how we can contrast these two types.

> Impact printers print by mechanical contact between print head and paper. **On the other hand,** non-impact printers do not require mechanical contact. Impact printers are noisy, **whereas** non-impact printers are silent.

Finally, we can add examples.

> The daisywheel printer **is an example of** an impact printer. **One type of** non-impact printer is a thermal printer.

Task 9

Another way to classify printers is by speed.

Study these facts about fast and slow printers.

Fast	Slow
usually print a line or even a page at a time	print a character at a time
used with mainframe computers	used with microcomputers
very expensive	inexpensive
e.g. laser	e.g. daisywheel

Now complete the blanks in this paragraph.

Printers can also be .... into .... and slow printers. Fast printers .... , whereas .... print a character at a time. Fast printers are normally used with mainframes. On the other hand .... with microcomputers. Fast printers are .... , whereas .... relatively inexpensive. One type of fast printer .... The daisywheel printer ....

Task 10

Study these facts about **plotters** *which are used for printing high-quality, detailed graphics such as are required in Computer Aided Design. Use these facts to write your own paragraph.*

It should include: a classifying sentence
a comparison and contrast of several points

Plotters	
drum plotters	*flatbed plotters*
paper is placed over a drum	paper is placed over a bed
the drum and pen movements are used to produce the drawing	only the pen is moved to produce the drawing
the drawing is produced in a series of small steps	the drawing is produced in a series of small steps
slow	slow

UNIT SIX
Storage Devices
Section One Reading Skills

Task 1

*Select the best two words from this list to complete this
sentence.*

permanent
volatile
limited
unlimited

A backing store provides more .... and almost

.... storage of information.

Now read Text 6.1 quickly to check if your answers are correct.

TEXT 6.1

Part of the main memory of a computer is **volatile** i.e. when the
computer is switched off, information in the memory is lost. Storage
devices are therefore used to provide a more permanent **backing store**.
They do this by storing the information on a storage medium such as
magnetic tape or **magnetic disc**. Storage devices are also being   5
developed which use a laser beam to store information on **video discs**.

Each group of information stored in a backing store, is referred to as a
file. The use of storage devices allows an almost unlimited number of files
to be stored. However, before a particular file can be used, it must be
transferred to the main memory.   10

The time taken to find a file and transfer it from the backing store to the
main memory, is called the **access time**. This affects the speed of the
computer system and is important in deciding which type of storage
device to use.

Task 2

Work in pairs, A and B. If working alone, do both parts.

Student A

Read Text 6.2 quickly to find out how a file is written to a disc. Then, using the list given below, complete boxes 2, 3, 6, 7 and 8 in Fig. 6.1.

Student B

Read Text 6.2 quickly to find out how a file is read from a disc. Then, using the list given below, complete boxes 2, 3, 9, 10 and 11 in Fig. 6.1.

a   The head moves to a track with empty sectors.
b   The formatting of the disc is verified.
c   The disc drive spins the disc at a high speed.
d   The address of the file is found from the catalogue.
e   The head moves across the surface of the disc, marking tracks and
     sectors.
f   The read/write head is brought very close to the disc surface.
g   The head moves to the correct track.
h   The name and address of the file is written into the catalogue.
i   The sectors pass under the head and the file is written onto them.
j   The file is read into the computer's memory.

Task 3

Share your answers with your partner to complete as much as you can of Fig. 6.1. Then, together, complete boxes 4 and 5, to show how a disc is formatted.

TEXT 6.2

A **magnetic disc** is a thin, flat circle of material coated with magnetic   15
oxide. By using magnetism, information can be stored on its surface.

However, a disc must be **formatted** before information can be put onto
it. This means that magnetic storage areas must be marked on its surface.
These storage areas are in the form of separate concentric circles called
tracks. Each track is subdivided into smaller areas known as **sectors**   20
(see Fig. 6.2).

A disc is referred to as a **single-sided disc** if it is formatted on one
surface only but, if it is formatted on both surfaces, it is referred to as a
double-sided disc.

FIG. 6.1

USING A DISC

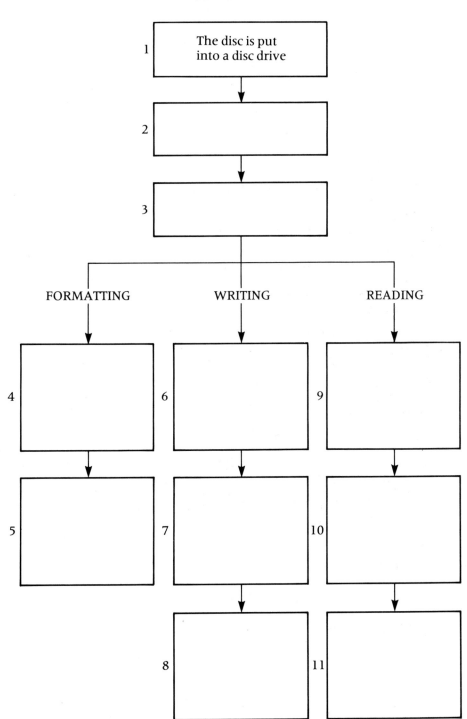

FIG. 6.2

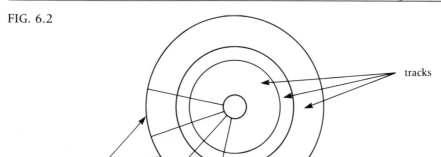

Formatting a disc makes it possible for each stored file to be given an   25
address i.e. a track and sector number. By using its address, any file can
be found directly, without passing through any other file. This is known
as **direct** or **random access** and enables files to be found quickly and
easily.

To use a disc, it is first put into a storage device called a **disc drive.**   30
Then, under the control of the computer, the disc drive spins the disc at a
high speed and brings a component called a **read/write head** very close
to its surface.

If the disc is being formatted, the read/write head moves across its
surface, magnetically marking tracks and sectors onto it. A special program   35
can be used to **verify** that a disc has been formatted correctly.

To write a file to a disc, the read/write head moves to a track which has
empty sectors. As these sectors pass under the read/write head, the file is
magnetically written onto them. The name and address of the file is also
written onto a special track which provides a **catalogue** or **directory**   40
of all the files on the disc.

To read a file from a disc, the read/write head first finds the address of
the required file from the catalogue. Then it moves directly to the correct
track. As the sectors containing the file pass under the read/write head, it
magnetically reads the file into the computer's memory. Reading a disc   45
does not affect the files stored on it.

Task 4

TEXT STUDY   Naming terms

Study these ways of introducing new terms.

These storage areas are in the form of separate concentric circles
called tracks. Each track is subdivided into smaller areas **known as**
sectors (see Fig. 6.2).
   A disc **is referred to as** a single-sided disc if it is formatted on
one surface only but, if it is formatted on both surfaces, it **is
referred to as** a double-sided disc.

Now complete the gaps in this text with these phrases and the correct terms.

is called   the address
is known as   formatting
is referred to as   direct or random access
                                                a file

Before information can be stored on a disc, magnetic areas have to be marked

on its surface. This .... (1). Once a

disc has been formatted, information can be written onto each sector. Each

group of stored information .... (2).

The position of each file on a disc .... (3)

of the file. Using the address, a file can be found directly without going through

other files. This .... (4).

Section Two   **Language Study**

Study these two actions:

1   Information is written onto the disc.
2   The disc is formatted.

Action **2** comes before action **1**. We can show the order of the actions using the
time words, **after** and **before**.

> **After** the disc is formatted, information is written onto it.
> **Before** information is written onto the disc, it is formatted.

To emphasise that one action comes before another, we can put the first action
in the perfect tense. Because the order is clear from the tense, we have a choice
of time words.

> **After/When/Once** the disc has been formatted, information is written
> onto it.

Now study these two actions:

3   The empty sectors pass under the read/write head.
4   The file is written onto the sectors.

Actions **3** and **4** happen at the same time. We can show this by linking them
with the time word **as.**

> **As** the empty sectors pass under the read/write head, the file is written
> onto them.

Note that commas are used between the actions in these examples because
time words come first in these sentences.

Task 5

Study these pairs of actions. Then link each pair using any suitable time word. Make any other necessary changes in the linked sentence.

1 The disc is put into a disc drive.
2 The drive spins the disc at a high speed.

3 The read/write head moves across the surface.
4 The head magnetically marks tracks and sectors onto the disc.

5 Formatting is completed.
6 The user verifies the disc is formatted correctly.

7 Empty sectors pass under the head.
8 A file is written onto the sectors.

9 The head finds the catalogue address of the file.
10 The head moves directly to the correct track.

Section Three Listening Skills

Task 6

Complete as much as you can of Table 6.1 using your own information.

TABLE 6.1

Discs: Technical details		
	Hard discs	*Floppy discs*
material	Aluminium	
sizes (diameter)	10″ approx	
tracks per surface		
type of computer used in		

Task 7

Now listen to the tape to check your answers and to complete any remaining blanks.

Task 8

Listen to the tape again to complete Table 6.2 of advantages and disadvantages.

TABLE 6.2

Discs: Advantages and Disadvantages			
	Hard discs	*Floppy discs*	*Winchester discs*
Advantages	Can hold large quantities of information		
Disadvantages		Information can be easily corrupted	

Task 9

Label these diagrams with the correct term from this list.

1 Disc pack
2 Floppy disc
3 Winchester

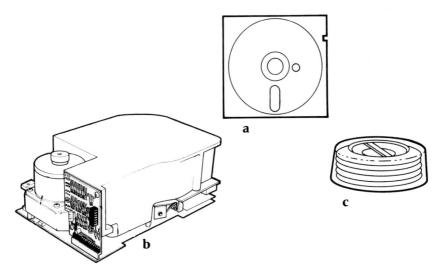

a

b

c

Section Four **Terminology**

Task 10

*Using information from this unit and Appendix 1, label
this diagram with these terms.*

a floppy disc   **d** disc pack
b non-exchangeable   **e** video disc
c exchangeable   **f** magnetic disc

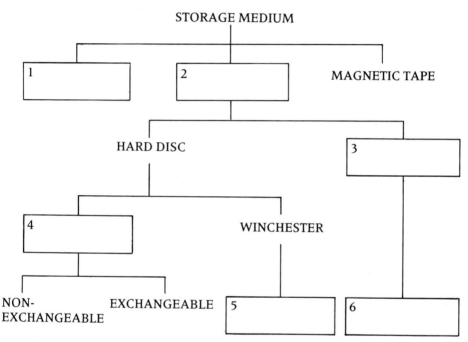

Task 11

*Match this list of terms from this unit with their
definitions. Then check your answers using Appendix 1.*

Terms		Definitions	
1	format	**a**	Check that a disc has been formatted correctly.
2	catalogue	**b**	Mark magnetic storage areas on the surface of a disc.
3	tracks	**c**	A list of the names and addresses of all the files on a disc.
4	sectors	**d**	Magnetic areas on a disc in the form of concentric circles.
5	verify	**e**	A set of hard discs stacked on one spindle.
6	disc pack	**f**	Subdivisions of tracks on a disc surface.

Section Five **Writing Skills**

Study this part of Table 6.2.

	Floppy Discs
Advantages	Small Cheap Fairly reliable Exchangeable
Disadvantages	Access is slower Easily damaged Information can be easily corrupted

Study this description of floppy discs which uses information from the table.

Floppy discs are small, cheap and fairly reliable. However, they are easily damaged. Information can be easily corrupted.

We can improve this description by adding listing sentences and further examples.

Floppy discs have several advantages. They are small, cheap and fairly reliable. **In addition,** they are exchangeable. **There are also some disadvantages.** They are easily damaged. **Moreover**, access is slower and information can be easily corrupted.

We can further improve the description by explaining difficult terms.

Floppy discs have several advantages. They are small, cheap and fairly reliable. In addition, they are exchangeable. **In other words**, they can be easily replaced by other discs. However, there are also some disadvantages. They are easily damaged. Moreover, access is slower and information can be easily corrupted, **that is,** it can be distorted or changed.

Task 12

Now study this information about magnetic tape cassettes as a backing store.

	Cassettes
Advantages	Formatting is not required Cheap Light and compact
Disadvantages	Very slow access time Unreliable

Write a paragraph comparing the advantages and disadvantages. Use listing sentences and explain **formatting** *and* **access time.**

Task 13

Look back at Table 6.2. Write your own paragraph about hard discs using the information in the table.

UNIT SEVEN
Central Processing Unit

Section One **Reading Skills**

Task 1

Try to answer these questions.

1 What are the two main components of the
  Central Processing Unit?
2 What is a chip?

*Read Text 7.1 quickly to check your answers or to find the
correct answer.*

TEXT 7.1

At the centre of the computer system is the CPU which can be considered
to be the 'brain' of the computer. Its main components are the central
processor and the main memory. The speed and capacity of these
components have been greatly improved with each new generation of
computers.   5

In the first generation, the central processor was built from electronic
valves which were rather unreliable. The second generation used
transistors. The third generation used integrated circuits. The fourth
generation of computers uses microprocessors. These are contained on
electronic **chips** which are slices of silicon with thousands of electronic   10
components and circuits engraved on them (see Fig. 7.1).

FIG. 7.1

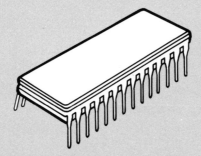

Early computers used magnetic cores in their main memory but fourth
generation computers use much smaller and more powerful electronic
memory chips.

Task 2

Read Text 7.1 again to complete this table.

Generation	Processor components
1 first	valves
2 second	
3 third	
4 fourth	

Task 3

Now work in pairs, A and B. If working alone, do both parts.

Student A

Read Text 7.2 to find the functions of each of these components:

1 control unit
2 registers
3 program counter
4 bus

Note your findings in Table 7.1.

Student B

Read Text 7.2 to find the functions of each of these components:

1 arithmetic and logic unit
2 registers
3 accumulator
4 clock

Note your findings in Table 7.1.

When you have completed your section of the table, share your findings with your partner so that you can both complete the table.

TEXT 7.2

The two main parts of the central processor are the Control Unit (**CU**) and the Arithmetic and Logic Unit (**ALU**).   15

The **control unit** controls all the other units in the computer system. It decodes the program instructions and makes sure they are carried out in the correct sequence. The **arithmetic and logic unit**, on the other hand, performs the calculations and data manipulation e.g. comparing, sorting   20
and combining data.

These units have small, short-term storage areas called **registers** which are used for special tasks. For example, the register in the CU known as the **program counter** is used to hold the address of the next instruction to be carried out. The register in the ALU known as the **accumulator** is   25
used to temporarily hold the data item currently being processed.

Each unit of the CPU is connected by a group of wires called a **bus**. There are data buses for carrying data from one unit to another, control buses for sending control signals to each unit and address buses for accessing each part of the main memory (see Fig. 7.2).   30

FIG. 7.2

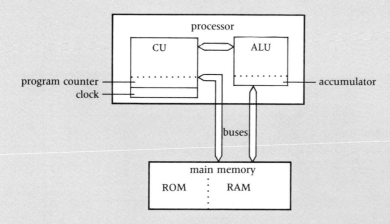

The power of the CPU is partly determined by its speed. This is controlled by a **clock** in the processor which sends out regular pulses to each unit to keep them in step. The clock pulse rate is measured in megahertz (MHz).

A computer can be made more powerful by connecting a second   35 processor to work in parallel with the first one. When computers are connected in a network configuration, the processing can be shared by the CPU's. This **distributed processing** makes the system much more powerful.

TABLE 7.1

Component	Function
1 control unit	
2 arithmetic and logic unit	
3 registers	
4 program counter	
5 accumulator	
6 bus	
7 clock	

Task 4

Label this diagram with these terms. Then compare your diagram with your neighbour's.

a processor
b accumulator
c main memory
d program counter
e ALU

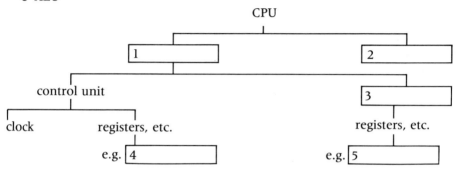

Section Two **Language Study**

Study this diagram.

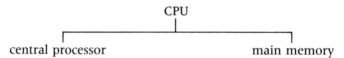

We can describe this diagram starting from the top, using these verbs and expressions.

| The CPU | consists of
comprises
is made up of
is composed of
can be divided into | the central processor and
the main memory. |

For example,

The CPU **comprises** the central processor and the main memory.
The CPU **is composed of** the central processor and the main memory.

We can also start at the bottom of the diagram with these verbs.

| The central processor
and the main memory | constitute
make up | the CPU. |

For example,

The central processor and the main memory **make up** the CPU.

If we do not want to mention all of the components of a system, we can use these verbs.

The central processor   includes   the ALU.
                           contains

Task 5

Describe this diagram from the top to the bottom. Then describe it from the bottom to the top.

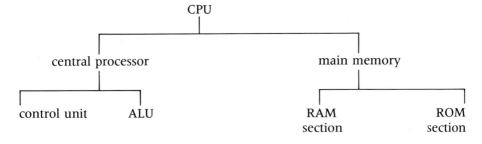

Task 6

Describe this diagram from the top to the bottom.

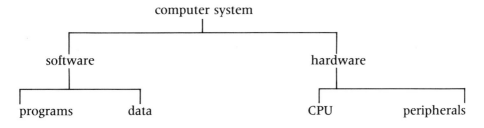

Section Three **Listening Skills**

Task 7

Study Fig. 7.3. Then listen to Part 1 of the tape. Write down the addresses of the cells described on the tape.

FIG 7.3

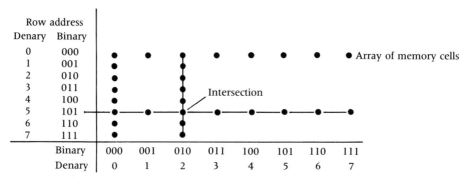

Column address

Task 8

This checklist indicates some of the features which distinguish the **RAM** section (Random Access Memory) from the **ROM** section (Read Only Memory).

Write YES or NO for each feature.

Feature	RAM	ROM
1 temporary storage		
2 permanent storage		
3 can be written to		
4 can be read from		
5 information lost when switched off		
6 information retained when switched off		
7 stores basic operating instructions		
8 stores user's programs and data		

Task 9

Now listen to Part 2 of the tape. Check your answers. Write in any missing answers.

Section Four **Terminology**

Computers translate all input into numbers according to a special code known as **ASCII** (American Standard Code for Information Interchange). The ASCII codes for some of the keyboard characters are given below.

CHARACTER	ASCII CODE	CHARACTER	ASCII CODE
0	00110000	A	01000001
1	00110001	B	01000010
2	00110010	C	01000011
3	00110011	D	01000100
4	00110100	E	01000101
5	00110101	F	01000110
6	00110110	G	01000111
7	00110111	H	01001000
8	00111000	I	01001001
9	00111001	J	01001010
:	00111010	K	01001011
;	00111011	L	01001100
<	00111100	M	01001101
=	00111101	N	01001110
>	00111110	O	01001111
?	00111111	P	01010000
@	01000000	Q	01010001

Task 10

With the help of Appendix 1, try to complete the gaps in this paragraph.
Each gap represents one missing word or number.

The numbers used in computers are called **binary** numbers. They are made up of the digits .... a .... and .... b .... Each .... c .... in a binary number is known as a **bit**. Each character used by a computer is represented by an .... d .... bit binary number. These numbers are given by an international code such as the **ASCII** (pronounced askey) **code**. For example, in the ASCII code, A is given the value 01000001. A **byte** is the number of .... e .... which make up one character. Hence, in the ASCII code .... f .... byte is equal to .... g .... bits.

Task 11

Affixes are often used in computer terminology. Knowing the meaning of common affixes may help you to work out what new terms mean.

Study these affixes of number, quantity and size.

Affix	Meaning	Affix	Meaning
mono bi deci (d) hexadeci kilo (K)	one two ten sixteen one thousand (in decimal system) $2^{10} = 1024$ (in binary system)	mega (M) multi milli (m) micro (μ) mini	very large one million (in decimal system) $2^{20} = 1048576$ (in binary system) many a thousandth a millionth, very small small

Now answer these questions.

1 A colour VDU can display graphics in many colours. What can a monochrome VDU show?
2 What can a bi-directional printer do?
3 The decimal system uses ten digits. How many digits does the hexadecimal system use?
4 Some storage devices can hold 100KB, i.e. one hundred times 1024 bytes of information. If a disc has a capacity of 10MB, how many bytes can it hold?
5 Which is bigger, a minicomputer or a microcomputer?
6 The .... nary system of counting uses two digits, 0 and 1.
7 Many terminals connected to one mainframe computer is known as a ....-user configuration.
8 A piece of film which can be used to store reduced images of hundreds of pages of print is known as a ....fiche.

Section Five **Writing Skills**

Task 12

Study this diagram which shows the components of a computer system.

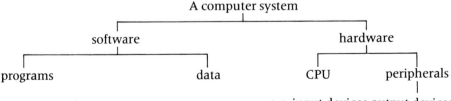

Here is one possible description.

> A computer system consists of software and hardware. Programs and data constitute the software. The CPU and peripherals make up the hardware. Peripherals include input and output devices.

We can improve the description by adding definitions of technical terms. For example,

> A computer system consists of software and hardware. Programs and data constitute the software. A program is a set of instructions telling the computer what operations and processes to carry out. Data is the information to be processed. The CPU and peripherals make up the hardware. The CPU is the 'brain' of the computer. Peripherals include input and output devices.

We can also add information on the function of certain components. For example,

> . . . Peripherals include input and output devices. Input devices are used to enter data of all kinds into the computer. Output devices are used to display the results obtained from the computer.

Task 13

Study this diagram which shows the components of the CPU. Write a detailed description of the CPU. Your description should include:

1   the components and how they relate to each other
2   definitions of difficult terms
3   the functions of important components

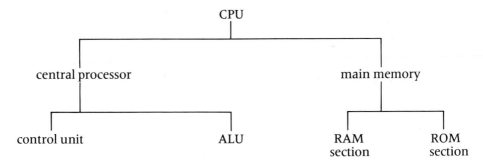

UNIT EIGHT
Data Communications Systems

Section One Reading Skills

Task 1

Try to answer these questions.

1 What is the purpose of a graphics terminal?
2 How can terminals be connected to a computer
   which is a long distance away?

*Now read Text 8.1 quickly to check your answers or to
find the correct answers.*

TEXT 8.1

A multi-user system is made up of a number of terminals sharing a
mainframe computer. Each **terminal** consists of at least one input device
and output device and allows the user to communicate with the computer.

There are a number of different types of terminals. For example, a   5
teletype terminal is made up of a keyboard and a printer which gives a
hardcopy output.

A **VDU terminal** has a keyboard and a VDU screen. It usually has its
own internal processor which deals with the input/output and editing of
data and is, therefore, referred to as an **intelligent terminal**.   10

A **graphics terminal** is similar to a VDU terminal but is specially
designed to display graphics such as pictures, maps, graphs, diagrams etc.
and has a lightpen attached to allow the user to 'draw' on the screen. It is
normally used for Computer Aided Design.

Often a mainframe computer and its terminals are situated a long   15
distance apart. They may be, for example, in different rooms, different
buildings, different cities or even different countries from each other.
These **remote access terminals** are connected to the mainframe computer by telecommunications links e.g. telephone lines.

Computers and terminals connected together using telecommunications   20
links form what is known as a **data communications** (or **datacomm**)
system.

Task 2

Read Text 8.1 again to complete this table.

Terminal	Components	Features
1 Teletype		
2 VDU		
3 Graphics		

Task 3

Now work in pairs, A and B. If working alone, do both parts.

Student A

Read Text 8.2 to find out the functions of each of these:

1 network
2 LAN
3 modem
4 communications satellite

Note your findings in Table 8.1.

Student B

Read Text 8.2 to find out the functions of each of these:

1 network
2 WAN
3 fibre optics cable
4 microwave radio

Note your findings in Table 8.1.

When you have completed your section of the table, share your findings with your partner so that you can both complete the table.

TABLE 8.1

Datacomm Systems	
Component	Function
1 Network	
2 LAN	
3 WAN	
4 Modem	
5 Fibre optics cable	
6 Microwave radio	
7 Communications satellite	

TEXT 8.2

Datacomm systems may also be formed from a number of computers and peripherals connected together in a network. This allows software and hardware to be shared by a large number of users over long distances. 25

A network which is contained in a relatively small area, such as an office building, factory site or university campus, is known as a **Local Area Network** or **LAN**. The two main types of LAN are **single cable networks** and **loop networks** (see Fig. 8.1).

FIG 8.1

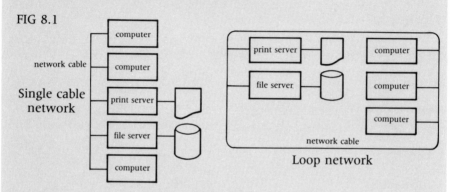

Single cable network

Loop network

In a single cable network, each computer 'listens' all the time for data 30 addressed to it and only transmits data when the network is quiet. A loop network, on the other hand, continuously circulates **data 'slots'** which can be filled with data. Data is transmitted by filling an empty slot with a 'packet' of data as the slot passes the transmitting device.

If the network is connected over a larger area it is called a **Wide Area** 35 **Network** or **WAN**. This may be linked using telephone lines. **Dedicated lines** are permanently connected to a system but **dialled lines** are only connected when needed. However, existing telephone lines are designed to carry analogue signals and not the digital signals used by computers. A special device is therefore needed at each end of the telephone line to 40 convert the signals to the correct form. This device is known as a **mod**ulator/**dem**odulator or **modem**. A special kind of modem known as an **acoustic coupler** has rubber cups into which an ordinary telephone can be plugged (see Fig. 8.2).

FIG. 8.2

Although this avoids having to make a special connection into the telephone system, it is more likely to suffer from corruption of data due to interference. 45

Modern telecommunications systems are being developed using **fibre optics cables**. These allow data to be transmitted as pulses of light along thin strands of glass (about the thickness of a human hair). In this way, data can be communicated at very high speed, measured in **bauds** i.e. bits per second. It also results in very low levels of interference. When telecommunications systems have been converted to digital systems using fibre optics cables and electronic telephone exchanges, modems will no longer be required. 50 55

Data can be communicated over long distances and over water by using **microwave radio** links. These transmit and receive high frequency microwave signals using small dish aerials. Since there must be a clear path between these aerials, they are usually situated at the top of high towers. 60

Data communications over very long distances can make use of **communications satellites** which are placed in fixed orbits above the Earth. The satellites receive signals from ground stations on Earth, amplify the signals, then re-transmit them to other ground stations which may be in another country or another continent. 65

The development of efficient data communications systems is an important aspect of the growth in information technology.

Section Two **Language Study**

Study these details about different types of terminals.

Terminal	Components	Features
Teletype	keyboard, printer	hardcopy output
VDU	keyboard, internal processor, VDU screen	allows data to be edited easily
Graphics	keyboard, internal processor, VDU screen, lightpen	used for Computer Aided Design

We can compare things which are similar as follows:

1   A VDU terminal **is similar to** a graphics terminal.
2   **Both** the VDU and the graphics terminal have VDU screens.
3   **Like** the teletype terminal, the VDU terminal has a keyboard.

We can contrast things which are different as follows:

4   A graphics terminal **is different from** a teletype terminal.

5   A teletype terminal can produce hardcopy output, **whereas** a graphics terminal is designed to display diagrams, etc. on a VDU screen.

6   **Unlike** a teletype terminal, a VDU terminal usually has an internal processor.

7   **In contrast to** ordinary terminals, intelligent terminals have their own internal processor.

Task 4

With the help of Texts 8.1, 8.2 and Appendix 1, write a sentence of comparison and contrast for each of these.

1   Dedicated lines, Dialled lines
2   Analogue signals, Digital signals
3   Local Area Networks, Wide Area Networks
4   Ordinary telephone cables, Fibre optics cables
5   Microwave radio links, Satellite links
6   Input devices, Output devices
7   Impact printers, Non-impact printers
8   Microcomputers, Mainframe computers

Section Three   **Listening Skills**

Task 5

Two important types of data communications services are known as **message switching services** and **videotex services**.

Listen to the tape to note three types of message switching services and two types of videotex services. Write your answers in Table 8.2.

TABLE 8.2

Message Switching
1
2
3
Videotex
4
5

Task 6

Listen to the tape again. Which form of data communications would be used for each of these needs?

1 To send a copy of a contract from one office to another.
2 To make travel information available to TV viewers in their own homes.
3 To send an enquiry quickly to an overseas company.
4 To send a photographic image from one police station to another.
5 To transfer money from one account to another from one's home.
6 To find out weather information before going on a journey.
7 To store messages from different sources for later collection.
8 To send copy from one newspaper printers to another in a form ready for printing.
9 To order and to pay for goods from one's home.

Section Four **Terminology**

Study these terms and their meanings.
  tele = *far, distant*
  data = *information*
  video = *seeing, visual*

Task 7

Study these definitions of different terms. Then complete the term defined with the correct word, **tele, data,** *or* **video**.

1 Pages of text broadcast as part of a TV signal.   .... **text**
2 A kind of storage device written to and read from by a laser beam.
                                                    .... **disc**
3 A large collection of information which can be searched to find a particular item.   .... **base**
4 A device that can send and receive data over long distances and produce a hardcopy printout.   .... **printer**
5 A form of data communications service which allows large amounts of information to be displayed on TV screens.   .... **tex**
6 The transfer of information over long distances using telephone lines, satellites, microwave radio, etc. .... **communications**
7 A kind of terminal consisting of a keyboard and a printer, used for sending messages over long distances. .... **type terminal**
8 A system for the transfer of information, formed by a computer and terminals connected by telecommunications links.
                              .... **communications system**
9 A system using teleprinters and the telephone system to provide information exchange all round the world.   .... **x**

Section Five **Writing Skills**

Task 8

Study this diagram. It shows an electronic mail system. Write a description of the system. Your description should include:

the components of the system
how they are connected
the function of the system and of the components
any special features the system has

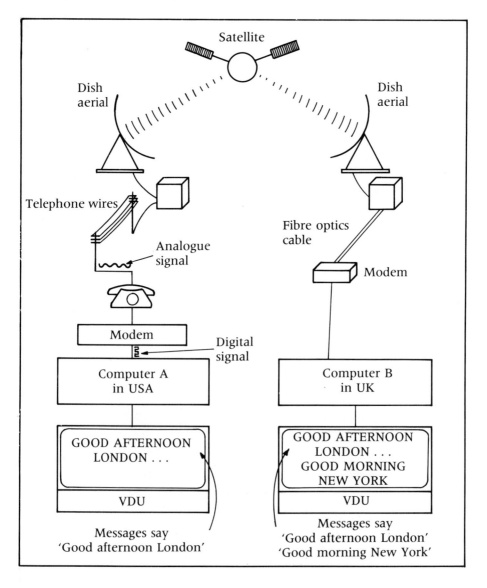

Task 9

Study this diagram. It shows a multi-user system. Compare and contrast this system with the electronic mail system you described in Task 8.

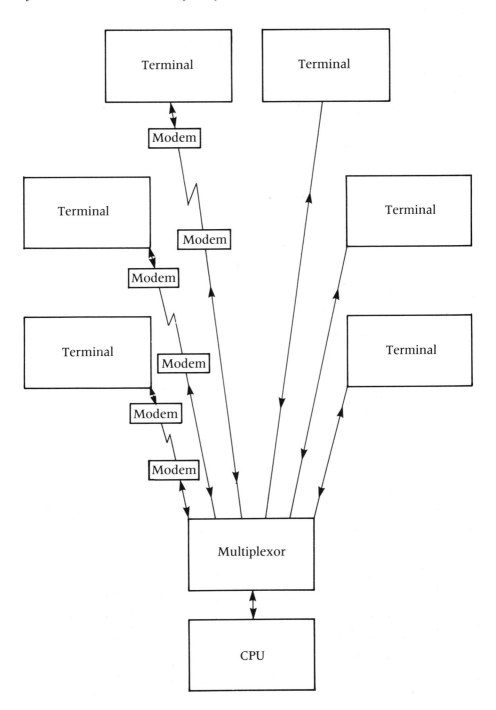

UNIT NINE
Computer Languages

Section One Reading Skills

Task 1

Try to answer these questions.

1 What languages do computers understand?
2 What is a high-level language?

Read Text 9.1 quickly to check your answers or to find the correct answers.

TEXT 9.1

Computers do not understand human languages such as English. The only languages they can understand directly are called **machine codes**. These consist entirely of binary numbers, therefore they are very difficult for humans to use. Writing a machine code program takes a very long time and is best left to experts. 5

A solution to the problem of writing programs is to use a computer language that is more easily understood by humans. Then, using a special program, the computer can translate them into machine code. For example, computer languages called **assembly languages** use mnemonics (abbreviations that are easy to remember) to represent 10 instructions e.g.

JMP   (**Ju**MP)
JSR   (**J**ump to **S**ub**R**outine)

Programs written in assembly languages are translated into machine code by a special program called an **assembler**. Since each line of an 15 assembly language program represents one machine code instruction, assembly languages and machine codes are known as **low-level languages**. Low-level languages allow programs to operate at high speed using the minimum of memory.

Although assembly languages simplify the writing of programs, they 20 are still quite complex. Computer languages which resemble English to some extent, are therefore often used. These languages are known as **high-level languages** because each instruction translates into many instructions of machine code. High-level languages make programs easier to write, modify and understand although the programs are executed 25 more slowly and use up more memory than programs written in low-level languages.

Task 2

Read Text 9.1 again to complete this table.

	Advantages	*Disadvantages*
high-level languages		
low-level languages		

Task 3

Read these facts about BASIC.

BASIC (**B**eginners **A**ll-purpose **S**ymbolic **I**nstruction **C**ode)

This language was written in 1964 as a teaching language. It is a general purpose language which is **interactive** i.e. data can be input while the program is running. It is very easy for beginners to learn and is very **user-friendly** e.g. it displays helpful error messages to tell the user when he has made a mistake. Although it is found on most microcomputers, there are many different dialects of BASIC. This makes it difficult to use the same program on two different makes of computer.

Study these notes about BASIC. What has been missed out? Why do you think this has been done?

language	BASIC
full title	Beginners All-purpose Symbolic Instruction Code
date	1964
use	general purpose
special features	easy to learn, user-friendly, interactive
other points	used on most microcomputers but many dialects exist

Task 4

Now work in pairs, A and B. If working alone, do both parts.

Student A	**Student B**
Read Text 9.2 to find out about these computer languages:	*Read Text 9.2 to find out about these computer languages:*
1 FORTRAN **2** ALGOL **3** LISP	**1** COBOL **2** PASCAL **3** LOGO
Note your findings in Table 9.1.	*Note your findings in Table 9.1.*

When you have completed your notes, share your information with your partner so that you can both complete the table.

TEXT 9.2

There are many different high-level languages. Each one has its advantages and disadvantages but some are better suited to particular types of work than others.   30

FORTRAN (FORmula TRANslator)

Written in 1956, this is one of the oldest languages. It is particularly suited to solving problems using formulas in science, engineering and mathematics. Although it is widely used in these fields, it is not as suitable for business applications and is more difficult to learn than some other languages. It was really designed for use on mainframe computers using   35
punched cards.

COBOL (COmmon Business Oriented Language)

This is another of the older languages dating from 1958. It is mainly used for business applications but is not as suitable for mathematics. This language is closer to English than the others and is therefore easier to read and write. However, programs written in COBOL tend to be very long.   40

ALGOL (ALGOrithmic Language)

This language was also written in 1958. It is suitable for business applications and is also good for mathematics. It is easy to understand because of its very clear structure.

PASCAL

This language, based on ALGOL, is named after the famous scientist Blaise Pascal. It is a more recent language, dating from 1973. It is a   45
general purpose language and is often used in colleges and universities as a teaching language. It is also commonly used for small business applications. Although it has a very clear structure, it is a little more difficult to learn than some other languages.

LISP (LISt Processing)

This language first made its appearance in 1959. It is designed for   50
processing lists and symbols and is used for artificial intelligence research. A LISP program can improve itself each time it is run. It is more flexible than other computer languages, however, it is difficult to learn.

LOGO

This is another modern language derived from LISP which made its appearance in 1969. It is a very simple language to learn and was designed to be used by very young children. It encourages a logical, structured use of language and has most often been used to control a special robot called a **turtle** and to teach mathematical concepts such as angles. 55

Other well known languages include FORTH, C, APL, ADA, PL/1, PROLOG, RPG, COMAL and APT. 60

TABLE 9.1

language	FORTRAN	COBOL	ALGOL	PASCAL	LISP	LOGO
date						
use						
special features						
other points						

Task 5

Using the completed Table 9.1, decide which language would best suit these needs. Then compare your answers with your neighbour.

1 A language for students learning to program for the first time.
2 A language for engineering students who have access to a university mainframe computer.
3 A language for software for an insurance company. The programs allow them to perform a wide range of mathematical calculations as well as keep files on policy holders.
4 A language which helps students with little computing experience to identify any mistakes they have made when keying in programs.
5 A language suitable for university level students and which has a wide range of applications.
6 A simple language for use on microcomputers.
7 A language used for writing software for a large commercial concern.
8 A language which allows data to be input while the program is running.
9 A language for scientists who have to use formulas frequently.
10 A general purpose language suitable for small businesses.
11 A language for controlling a simple robot.
12 A language for research in artificial intelligence.

Section Two **Language Study**

Study these ways of linking a favourable point and a less favourable point.

Favourable	*Less Favourable*
FORTRAN is widely used in engineering	FORTRAN is not as suitable for business applications
Assembly language is simpler than machine code	Assembly language is still quite complex

Although FORTRAN is widely used in engineering, it is not as suitable for business applications.

Even though assembly language is simpler than machine code, it is still quite complex.

We can also use **although** and **even though** between the points.

FORTRAN is not as suitable for business applications **although** it is widely used in engineering.

Assembly language is still quite complex **even though** it is simpler than machine code.

Task 6

Link each favourable point from Column A with a less favourable point from Column B. Then join the points together using any of the ways described in this section.

A	**B**
1 BASIC is found on most microcomputers	a FORTRAN is one of the oldest computer languages
2 PASCAL has a very clear structure	b High-level languages cannot be understood directly by computers
3 High-level languages can be easily understood by humans	c Machine code is very difficult to read and write
4 Machine code can be processed very quickly	d There are many different dialects of BASIC
5 FORTRAN is widely used in engineering	e PASCAL is more difficult to learn than BASIC

Section Three **Listening Skills**

Task 7

Fig. 9.1 shows the difference between compiling and interpreting a program. Using it, try to write a brief explanation of this difference.

FIG. 9.1

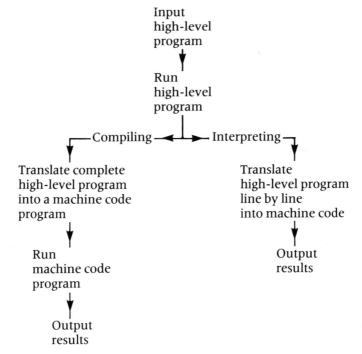

Task 8

Now listen to the tape. Compare your explanation with the information given on the tape. Try to improve your explanation.

Task 9

Listen to the tape again and complete this table.

	Advantages	*Disadvantages*
Compiling (mainly mainframes)		
Interpreting (mainly micros)		

Section Four **Terminology**

Task 10

Some terms are made up by taking letters from each word in a title.
Normally the first letter or letters are used. For example,

ROM = Read Only Memory

Now write out in full the meaning of each of these terms.

1	ASCII	6	pixel
2	LISP	7	FORTRAN
3	RAM	8	PROM
4	BASIC	9	COBOL
5	bit	10	CAD

Check your answers in Appendix 1.

Section Five **Writing Skills**

Task 11

A **flowchart** is a diagram that shows in what order different steps of a
process are carried out. Programmers often use flowcharts when planning
a program.

Study the symbols used in flowcharts, shown in Fig. 9.2.

FIG. 9.2   symbol   example

START or STOP (Start)

INPUT or OUTPUT   Key in any number

OPERATION/ PROCESS   Add A and B

DECISION   Is A less than B?

Now study this flowchart. It shows how tax is calculated on pay.

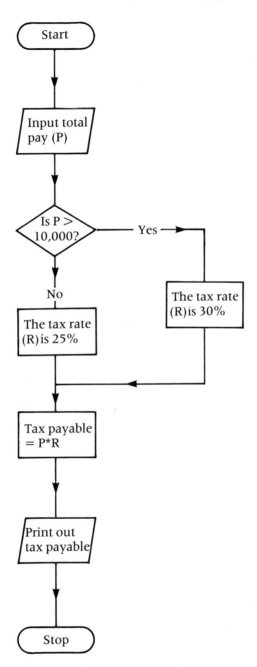

We can explain the flowchart like this.

First the total pay is input. If the pay is greater than 10,000, the tax rate is 30%. If the pay is not greater than 10,000, the tax rate is 25%. Tax payable is calculated by multiplying pay by the tax rate. Finally the tax payable is printed out.

Task 12

This flowchart shows how hotel bills can be calculated.
Write your own explanation of the flowchart.

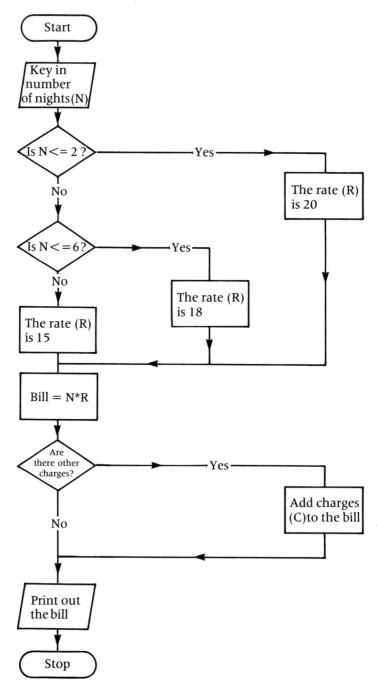

UNIT TEN
Software Systems

Section One Reading Skills

Task 1

Try to answer these questions.

1 What is a program library?
2 What is a payroll program for?

*Read Text 10.1 quickly to check your answers or to find
the correct answers.*

TEXT 10.1

The information used with computers is known as **software** and includes
programs and data. **Programs** are sets of instructions telling the computer
what operations have to be carried out and in what order they should be
done.

Specialised programs which enable the computer to be used for   5
particular purposes are called **applications programs**. A collection of
these programs kept in backing store, form what is known as a **program
library**.

There are two different types of applications programs; namely custom
programs and applications packages.   10

Custom programs are designed to suit a particular situation and are
usually written by the user himself. **Applications packages**, however,
are more general and are purchased complete with extensive documentation explaining how to use them for particular purposes. Common
applications packages include **payroll programs** for calculating   15
employees' wages, **database programs** for information retrieval, **word
processor programs** for text manipulation and **spreadsheet programs**
for financial planning.

Integrated packages have a number of programs combined in one
package so that the same data can be shared by them all.   20

Applications programs are usually stored on disc and loaded into the
main memory when required. However, they can also be put onto ROM
chips to make them immediately available to the user.

Task 2

Read Text 10.1 again to complete this diagram.

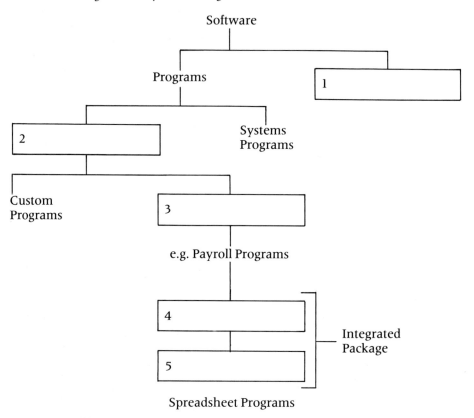

Task 3

Work in pairs, A and B. If working alone, do both parts.

Student A

Read Text 10.2 to find out about these types of systems programs:

1 operating system
2 database management system

Note your findings in Fig. 10.1.

Student B

Read Text 10.2 to find out about these types of systems programs:

1 utility programs
2 language translators

Note your findings in Fig. 10.1.

When you have completed your notes, share your information with your partner so that you can both complete Fig. 10.1.

FIG. 10.1 SYSTEMS PROGRAMS

OPERATING SYSTEMS
main function _____

examples of functions _____

LANGUAGE TRANSLATORS
function _____

examples _____

UTILITY PROGRAMS
function _____

examples _____

DATABASE MANAGEMENT
SYSTEMS
function _____

TEXT 10.2

The programs which control the basic functions of a computer system are known as **systems programs**. They include the operating system, utility (or service) programs, language translators and database management systems. 25

The **operating system** is the most important type of systems software. It consists of a group of programs designed to manage and co-ordinate all the hardware and software of a computer system as efficiently as possible and to provide communications between the computer and the user. It is a very complex piece of software which performs many different functions such as controlling the operation of the disc drives, displaying prompts and cursors, keeping the system running if an error occurs in a program, checking the input of identification numbers and passwords and keeping a log of terminals used in a multi-user system. 30 35

The operating system must be compatible with the central processor and is usually supplied by the computer manufacturer. If it is stored on ROM chips, it comes into operation as soon as the computer is switched on. Often, however, it is stored on a disc and must be loaded into the main memory before any other operations can be carried out. Table 10.1 shows some common operating systems. 40

TABLE 10.1

System	Meaning	Type of computer
CP/M	Control Program for Microcomputers	Micro
MSDOS	Micro Soft Disc Operating System	Micro
UNIX	– – – – –	Mini
VME	Virtual Machine Environment	Mainframe

Utility programs are small systems programs which perform one simple task. Some utilities perform common tasks known as **housekeeping routines**. These include copying files from tape to disc, sorting data into alphabetical or numerical order, merging or combining two or more files to make one larger file, cataloguing a disc by displaying the names of the stored files on a VDU screen and performing **screen dumps** i.e. copying VDU screen displays to a printer.   45

An important utility is the **editor**. It allows the user to make changes to programs and data. This would include adding new information, deleting unwanted information and correcting existing information.   50

Language translators form a third type of systems program. Their function is to translate programs written in various computer languages into machine code. They also perform functions such as giving error messages if syntax errors occur in a program and displaying listings of programs on a VDU screen when requested. Language translators include assemblers, compilers and interpreters.   55

A **database management system (DBMS)** is a set of systems programs which allow the data from a database to be used by a number of different applications programs. It includes facilities for ensuring the independence, integrity and security of data.   60

Task 4

Working together with your partner, complete this diagram using the correct terms from Text 10.2.

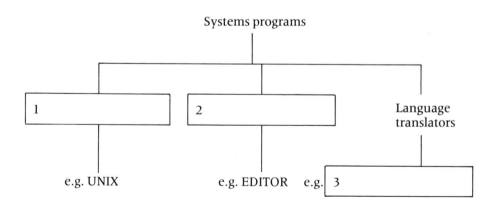

Section Two **Language Study**

Study these statements:

1 Integrated packages have a number of programs combined in one package.
2 Applications programs can be put onto ROM chips.

We can add a purpose to each statement in two ways:

1 Integrated packages have a number of programs combined in one package **so that** the same data can be shared by them all.
2 Applications programs can also be put onto ROM chips **to** make them immediately available to the user.

Task 5

Link each statement in Column A with a purpose from Column B.

A	**B**
1 Applications programs are designed for general use	a produce detailed graphics
2 Custom programs are sometimes specially written by the user	b provide easy access to a range of programs
3 A program library is often kept in backing store	c the user can 'draw' on the screen
4 A word processor justifies each line of text	d suit a particular situation
5 A high resolution monitor is used	e they can be used in many different situations
6 A graphics terminal includes a lightpen	f they will form a straight edge

Task 6

Write your answers to Task 5 as complete sentences. For example,

1e Applications programs are designed for general use so that they can be used in many different situations.

Section Three **Listening Skills**

Task 7

*Study Fig. 10.2. It shows the personnel employed in
a large computer installation. Try to guess some of
their duties.*

   FIG. 10.2

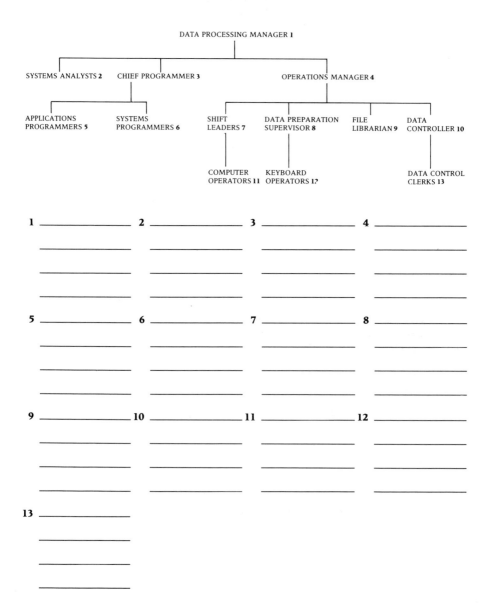

1 _____ 2 _____ 3 _____ 4 _____

   _____   _____   _____   _____

   _____   _____   _____   _____

   _____   _____   _____   _____

5 _____ 6 _____ 7 _____ 8 _____

   _____   _____   _____   _____

   _____   _____   _____   _____

   _____   _____   _____   _____

9 _____ 10 _____ 11 _____ 12 _____

   _____   _____   _____   _____

   _____   _____   _____   _____

   _____   _____   _____   _____

13 _____

   _____

   _____

   _____

Task 8

Work in pairs, A and B. If working alone, do both parts.

Student A

Listen to the tape to find out the duties of these personnel.

1 processing manager
2 applications programmer
3 data preparation supervisor
4 data control clerk

Note your findings on Fig. 10.2.

Student B

Listen to the tape to find out the duties of these personnel.

1 systems analyst
2 systems programmer
3 computer operator
4 file librarian

Note your findings on Fig. 10.2.

When you have completed your section of Fig. 10.2, share your findings with your partner so that you can both complete it.

Section Four **Terminology**

Task 9

Study the flowchart for calculating tax on pay which is shown in Task 11, Unit 9. Now study this BASIC program developed from the flowchart.

```
10  REM Tax calculation
20  INPUT P
30  IF P>10000 GOTO 60
40  LET R=25/100
50  GOTO 70
60  LET R=30/100
70  PRINT P*R
80  END
```

This program contains some BASIC commands.

Study them and their meanings.

Command	Meaning
REM	Remark, a reminder to the programmer about the purpose of a program.
INPUT	Waits for the user to input or enter data from the keyboard.
IF	A decision statement. It tests to see if a condition is true.
GOTO	Go to the line number given. A way of directing a program forward or back.
LET	A way of giving a value to a variable.
PRINT	Displays the result of a calculation on the VDU screen.
END	Marks the end of the program.

We can explain this program line by line.

Try to complete the blanks in the explanation.

10 This program is for .... tax.

20 .... the amount of pay.

30 .... the pay is greater than 10,000, go forward to line 60.

40 .... the tax rate equal 25%.

50 .... forward to line 70.

60 Let the tax rate .... 30%.

70 Display the .... of multiplying pay by tax rate.

80 This is the .... of the program.

Section Five **Writing Skills**

Task 10

Study this description of a Systems Analyst.

The job of a Systems Analyst is to study existing systems and advise on how they can be put onto a computer. A Systems Analyst is responsible for designing new systems and putting them into operation. His or her work may also involve training staff and preparing instruction manuals.

Using your notes from Section Three together with any other information you can find, write a similar description of the work of a Programmer (both Systems and Applications).

UNIT ELEVEN
Computer Applications

Section One Reading Skills

Task 1

*List some of the computer hardware you might find in a
doctors' surgery. Then read Text 11.1 to check how many
of your guesses are correct.*

TEXT 11.1

A typical computer application can be illustrated by considering how a
computer system might be used in a doctors' surgery.

Microcomputers would be used since they are more than powerful
enough for any functions likely to be required.

The main input device would be a QWERTY keyboard, perhaps with an   5
integral numeric keypad. A mouse might also be used for selecting
functions.

A monitor would be used for displaying output but an NLQ dot matrix
printer would be required to give a hardcopy printout of lists, summaries,
prescriptions, accounts, graphs etc. A daisywheel printer would also be   10
useful for printing letters and reports.

Programs and data would be stored on disc. If floppy discs were used, a
dual disc drive would be useful for making backup copies of important
data. However, a Winchester would provide faster access to large amounts
of information.   15

Each doctor and the receptionist could have a micro connected in a
network configuration. If a modem was used, the system could be
connected by telephone lines to a mainframe computer at a hospital. This
would provide the doctors with access to large databases of research
information.   20

This is an example of a system which could be expanded and adapted as
required.

Task 2

Work in pairs, A and B. If working alone, do both parts.

Student A

Read Text 11.2 to identify the type of program used for each of these tasks in the surgery.

1 maintaining patient files
2 writing repeat prescriptions
3 recording appointments
4 preparing visuals for medical research

Student B

Read Text 11.2 to identify the type of program used for each of these tasks in the surgery.

1 identifying categories of patient
2 checking a prescription for drug interactions
3 preparing and addressing reminders
4 preparing accounts

When you have finished, share your findings with your partner.

TEXT 11.2

The software would probably consist of integrated applications packages which might include a database program, a word processor program and a graphics program. A diary planner program and a drug interaction program would also be useful.   25

The database program would be used to store patient files containing records of each patient. Each record would give details such as the patient's name, address, telephone number, date of birth and medical history. It may also include dates for further appointments.   30

The doctor could instruct the program to search for a particular patient's record which would then be displayed on a VDU screen. He could then update the record by inputting new information using a keyboard.

Using the database program, the records could be automatically sorted into any order e.g. alphabetical order, and classified into various categories.   35
This would enable the doctor to quickly identify groups of patients, for example, men over forty with high blood pressure. Lists of any required category could be printed out using a printer.

Repeat prescriptions could also be stored on the database and printed out when required. The program could be designed to limit the number of   40
times the repeat prescription would be printed without further instructions from the doctor. A drug interaction program would check each prescription so that drugs which interacted badly with each other would not be prescribed.

The diary planner program could be used to keep an appointments diary for each doctor. The receptionist could then print out lists of appointments and house calls. Each week, summaries could be printed of the number of patients seen, etc.   45

The receptionist could use the word processor program to store standard letters which would be printed out when required. These might include reminder notices for check-ups, vaccinations, etc.   50

The data from the database could be combined with the standard letters to personalise them by automatically inserting the name, address etc. in the correct place. This facility is known as **mail merging**. The same data could be used by the database program to print out address labels for the envelopes.   55

The doctor could use the graphics program to display graphs of the data stored in the database. This would help him to carry out medical research and analysis.

Other software such as accounts packages could be used to calculate salaries and the amount spent on drugs etc. This software could gradually be improved and expanded to suit the needs of the doctors.   60

Task 3

Work together to label this diagram with the names of the types of programs used for each of the tasks illustrated.

1. Maintaining medical records

Surname	First Names	
Age Sex	Marital Status	
Occupation		
Present Complaint		

2. Writing repeat prescriptions Checking for drug interactions

Rx

Tab Dihydrocodeine B.P. 30 mgm
Mitte 100 (one hundred tabs)
Sig. 2 tablets, 6 hrly for pain, p.c.

3. Keeping appointments diary

Dr Ginn
9.15 Mrs Watt
9.25 Mr Cook
9.35 Mr Stott

4. Writing and addressing reminder letters

Dear Mrs Hall,
John is due to have his
pre-school booster.
Please call in on Monday
24th. at 3.45.

5. Preparing visuals for medical research

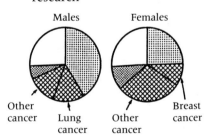

Males   Females

Other cancer   Lung cancer   Other cancer   Breast cancer

6. Calculating salaries, accounts, etc.

Salaries,   May
Dr Ginn   £35,000
Dr Wood   £40,000
Dr Wren   £17,000

Section Two **Language Study**

Compare these statements.

1 Computers **make** the doctor's work much easier.
2 Computers **would make** the doctor's work much easier.

Statement **1** describes a surgery where computers are in use.

Statement **2** describes a surgery where computers are not yet in use but may be used in the future.

We use statements like this when we talk about possible future plans.

Study these further examples.

3 The doctor **can** instruct the program to search for a patient's record.
   (This is possible now. The computer is in use.)
4 The doctor **could** instruct the program to search for a patient's record.
   (This will be possible in the future if a computer is installed).

Task 4

*Study this list of tasks a microcomputer could perform in
an office.*

1 Produce company documents
2 Find files quickly
3 Ensure the accounts are accurate
4 Compare sales from year to year
5 Keep a record of all customers
6 Produce diagrams for company documents
7 Keep a record of stock
8 Calculate tax on the price of goods

Now study these types of programs available for the microcomputer.

a word processor
b database
c accounts
d graphics
e spreadsheet

Find the type of program from this list which would be used for each of these tasks.
For example,

A word processor program would be used to produce company
documents.

Section Three **Listening Skills**

Task 5

*Study Fig. 11.1, which shows a medical record card.
Then, answer these questions.*

1 What is a field?
2 What is a key field?

FIG. 11.1

Key field

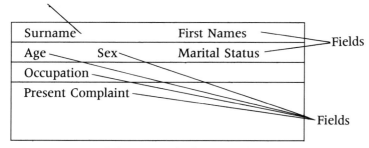

Listen to Part 1 of the tape to check your answers.

Task 6

Work in pairs, A and B. If working alone, do both parts.

Student A

*Listen to Part 2 of the tape
and note the disadvantages
of a manual filing system.
Note your findings in Table
11.1.*

Student B

*Listen to Part 2 of the tape
and note the advantages of
a computer database
program. Note your
findings in Table 11.1.*

*When you have completed your section of the table, share your information with
your partner so that you can both complete the table.*

TABLE 11.1

Manual filing	Computer database program
disadvantages	advantages

Section Four **Terminology**

Study these terms used with database programs.

create
update
delete
edit
sort
merge
search
field
key field
wildcard

If you are not sure of the meaning of any of these terms, listen again to the tape for Section Three.

Task 7

Now complete these sentences by using each term correctly. You may change the form of the term.
For example,

> Files can be **updated** by adding new information.

1 We can .... files by correcting items in the records.
2 One advantage of a database program is that it can ....
    on several fields at one time.
3 We use .... characters to locate records when information
    is incomplete.
4 .... a file means designing it for the first time.
5 Records can be .... quickly either alphabetically or numerically,
    using any field.
6 The .... of a record has to be unique.
7 Common .... in a doctor's records would include age, sex,
    problems and treatment.
8 When a worker leaves a company, his record will be ....
9 When a new patient registers, the files must be ....
10 A number of files can be .... to create larger files.

Section Five **Writing Skills**

Task 8

Study this table of the advantages and disadvantages of manual filing and computer database systems.

	Manual	Computer database
Advantages	Cheap to set up	Cheap to run Fast, automatic sorting Fast, automatic search Complex searches on more than one field and for general or incomplete information Records cannot be lost easily Large amounts of information can be stored in a small space
Disadvantages	Expensive to run Needs a lot of space Files have to be stored in one order Records can be mislaid Updating and other changes mean rewriting the file'	Expensive to set up Breakdowns can occur Security of information has to be ensured

Now write a comparison and contrast of the two systems. Your answers to Tasks 6 and 7 may be helpful.

UNIT TWELVE
Applications Programs
Section One **Reading Skills**

Task 1

Try to answer these questions.

1 Where can applications programs be stored?
2 What is a menu?

*Read Text 12.1 quickly to check your answers or to find
the correct answers.*

TEXT 12.1

Applications programs can be held in backing store on a magnetic disc or
tape. However, before a program can be put into operation, it must first
be loaded into the RAM area of the computer's main memory. This must
be done each time a program is used.

Alternatively, applications programs can be stored on ROM chips. These   5
are plugged into sockets in the ROM area of the computer's main
memory. Since the programs are resident in the main memory, the user
can put any program into operation immediately, by inputting a special
command.

Some applications programs are command driven and others are menu   10
driven. When a **command driven** program is being executed, it is
controlled by commands keyed in by the user. A **menu driven** program,
however, displays a **menu** or list of choices, on the VDU screen.

```
              MENU
    1.    Load Text
    2.    Run Program
    3.    Save Text

    Input your choice (1-3)
```

The user controls the program by choosing one item from the menu.   15
This can be done using the keyboard, a mouse, a lightpen or some other
input device.

Task 2

Work in pairs. If working alone, do both parts.

Student A   **Student B**

*Read Text 12.2 to find out   Read Text 12.2 to find out
about these features of   about these features of
word processing programs.   word processing programs.*

1 word-wrap   1 editing facilities
2 embedded codes   2 spelling checker
3 justification   3 mail merging

*When you have finished, share your information with your
partner so that you both understand these features.*

TEXT 12.2

Word processing programs are used for the preparation and editing of
letters and other documents.

The text is keyed in using the keyboard but it is not printed onto paper   20
directly. Instead, it is displayed on the VDU screen and stored in the
computer's memory. This allows the text to be edited before it is printed
out in its final form.

As the text is being input, if there is not enough space left on a line to
display the next complete word, it is automatically moved to the   25
beginning of the next line. This **word-wrap** facility makes inputting a
text much easier than using a typewriter where the typist has to judge
when to begin a new line.

Useful information, such as the number of words in the text, the
amount of space remaining in the memory and the typing speed, can be   30
displayed on the screen while the text is being keyed in.

Various **editing facilities** are also available. After the cursor has been
moved to the required position, characters can be deleted or inserted.
When this happens, the rest of the text is automatically moved along to
keep the spacing of the text correct. Other facilities allow sections of   35
the text to be moved or copied to another position without having to key
in the characters again. There may also be a facility for the program to
search for all the occurrences of a given word and replace it with another
word.

By inserting special command codes into the text (**embedded codes**),   40
the user can control how it will be printed out e.g. words may be
underlined, printed in bold type or in italics. It may also be possible to

create an index by marking words with embedded codes. After the text has been keyed in, the program will automatically print out an index of the marked words and page references of where they occur in the text.   45

Some word processors have a built-in **spelling checker** which will compare words in the text with a dictionary of words in the computer's memory. If an unknown word or spelling is found, it will be indicated to the user.

When the text is complete, it can be permanently stored in a backing   50
store. This allows the text to be used again at a different time without having to retype it. It may also be possible to merge two or more stored texts to give one longer text.

The text can be printed out on paper using a printer. Before this is done, the user can determine the print layout. This includes deciding on   55
such things as page numbering, line spacing, size of margins and **justification** i.e. whether to have the left or right edge of the text straight.

Mail merging facilities combine a database with the word processor. This enables names and addresses stored in the database to be automat-   60
ically inserted into the text. In this way, standard letters can be addressed to a number of different people.

Task 3

Each of these figures illustrates a feature of word processing.

Label each figure with the correct term from this list.

word-wrap   spelling checker
editing facilities   embedded codes
mail merging   left and right justification

1

An ordinary typewriter cannot do this but a word processor can automatically adjust the spacing of the text so that both edges are straight.

2

Before: This featur compairs words in the text with a dictionary stored
             in the memory.
After: This feature compares words in the text with a dictionary
             stored in the memory.

3

Before: It is very difficult to do on a typewriter without retyping the
             entire line.
After: It is very difficult to do this on a typewriter without retyping
             the line.

4

Dear ....

Mr E.H. Jones
Winspur Avenue

You have been specially selected
from all the residents of ....
.... to receive an offer
which is unrepeatable.

Mrs F. Jones
3 Station Road

5

These features control the way *the text* will be printed out.

6

Typewriter: This feature makes keying in much simpler on a word pro
cessor than on a typewriter.

**Word
processor:** This feature makes keying in much simpler on a word
processor than on a typewriter.

Section Two **Language Study**

Task 4

*Fill in each space in this description with a suitable
time word from this list.*

when   before   after   until   once   as

.... 1 .... a text is being keyed in, the screen displays

the number of bytes remaining. The user can continue to input text

.... 2 .... no more space

remains in the memory. .... 3 .... this happens, the

text must be transferred to backing store .... 4 ....

more text is input.

.... 5 .... the text has been

completed, it should be saved. .... 6 .... printing is done, the user

should decide on the layout. A spelling checker can be used to check for

errors .... 7 .... the final version is printed.

.... 8 .... the layout has been

chosen and the spelling checked, the text can be printed out.

Task 5

Fill in each space in this description with one word.

Word processors allow texts .... 1 .... be produced
more quickly .... 2 .... ordinary typewriters. Mistakes
can .... 3 .... corrected easily and even the final
layout .... 4 .... the text can be planned before
printing. .... 5 .... texts can be stored ....
6 .... a backing store, they .... 7 .... be used
again and again. .... 8 .... avoids unnecessary work.
In ....9 .... way word processors simplify the work
.... 10 .... writing and editing texts.

Task 6

Fill in each space in this description with a suitable preposition.

Check your answers after completing Section 3.

Spreadsheet programs are used .... 1 .... business
people .... 2 .... financial planning. A spreadsheet is
like a very large sheet of paper divided .... 3 ....
vertical columns and horizontal rows. Each column is labelled ....
4 .... a number .... 5 .... easy reference.
Because the spreadsheet is large, only part of it can be displayed
.... 6 .... a time but it is simple for the user to go
quickly .... 7 .... one section .... 8 ....
another.

Section Three **Listening Skills**
Task 7

Study Fig. 12.1. Then try to answer these questions.

1 What sort of person would use such information?
2 What is the relationship between column C and columns A and B?
3 What appears in position B2?
4 What should appear in position C1?

FIG. 12.1

		A	B	C
1		cost per item	number of items	
2	C30 cassettes	0.65	100	65.00
3	C60 cassettes	0.90	300	270.00
4	C90 cassettes	1.00	280	280.00

Task 8

Now listen to the tape to check your answers.

Task 9

Study Fig. 12.1. Now write down the formula which should be keyed into the following cells to give the results shown in Fig. 12.2. The first one has been done for you.

1 D2 = A2 * B2
2 D4 =
3 E2 =
4 E5 =

FIG. 12.2

	A *Cost per item*	**B** *Quantity ordered*	**C** *Discount per 100*	**D** *Total cost*	**E** *Total cost less discount*
1					
2 C30's	0.65	100	10.00	65.00	55.00
3 C60's	0.90	500	15.00	450.00	375.00
4 C90's	1.00	700	20.00	700.00	560.00
5			Total	1215.00	990.00

Section Four **Terminology**

Task 10

Study these groups of terms you have met in this book. Try to find a suitable label for each group. For example,

Printer
VDU   = Output devices
Voice synthesiser
Graphics tablet

1	BASIC COBOL PASCAL FORTRAN	2	Thermal Dot-matrix Ink-jet Laser	3	Videotex Teletext Viewdata
4	CPU VDU Keyboard	5	Magnetic tape Magnetic disc Video disc	6	Compiler Interpreter Assembler

Task 11

This task is more difficult. Try to recall terms which will fit into each of these groups.

1 Computer personnel   **2** Software

_____   _____
_____   _____
_____   _____
_____   _____

3 Terminals   **4** Peripherals

_____   _____
_____   _____
_____   _____
_____   _____

5 System
    configurations

_____
_____
_____
_____

Section Five **Writing Skills**

Task 12

List the similarities and differences between a word processor and a typewriter. List the main advantages of a word processor. Then write a short text comparing and contrasting the typewriter and word processor.

Appendices

1 Glossary

access time *n*
time taken to find and transfer information to and from memory (6,   1)

accumulator *n*
special register in the processor used for storing the data item currently being processed (7,   1)

acoustic coupler *n*
type of modem which allows an ordinary telephone receiver to be used for connecting a computer to the telephone system (8,   1)

ADC *n*
Analogue to **D**igital **C**onverter (4,   1)

address *n*
code number giving the position of stored information (6,   1)

ALGOL *n*
ALGOrithmic **L**anguage High-level language suitable for business and mathematics (9,   1)

ALU *n*
Arithmetic and **L**ogic **U**nit (7,   1)

analog(ue) signal *n*
signal which changes in a continuous manner (4,   1)

analogue to digital converter *n*
component which changes analogue signals into digital signals (4,   1)

applications package *n*
applications program complete with documentation which can be used in a variety of situations (10,   1)

applications program *n*
program designed to perform a particular type of function (10,   1)

applications programmer *n*
person who writes and modifies applications programs (10,   3)

arithmetic and logic unit *n*
part of the processor which performs all the processing, i.e. data manipulations and calculations (7,   1)

ASCII *adj*
American **S**tandard **C**ode for **I**nformation **I**nterchange (7,   4)

ASCII code *n*
standard code which represents each character by an 8 bit binary number (7,   4)

assembler *n*
systems program used to translate an assembly language program into machine code (9,   1)

assembly language *n*
low-level computer language which uses mnemonics for instructions (9,   1)

auto-repeating *adj*
automatically keeps performing the same function again and again (1,   1)

back up *v adj*
copy files from a disc onto a second disc (6,   3)

backing store *n*
store for programs and data which are not being used immediately (6,   1)

backup copy *n*
copy of a disc, usually kept in case the original disc is damaged (6,   3)

bar code *n*
series of black and white lines of varying thickness used to identify items (4,   3)

bar code reader *n*
input device used to read bar codes (4,   3)

BASIC *n*
Beginners **A**ll-purpose **S**ymbolic **I**nstruction **C**ode General purpose high-level language found on most microcomputers (9,   1)

baud *n*
the rate of data transmission 1 baud = 1 bit per second (8,   1)

binary *adj*
number system which only uses two digits, i.e. 0 and 1 (7,   4)

bit *n*
BInary digi**T**, i.e. 0 or 1 (7,   4)

bug *n*
mistake in a program or fault in a piece of equipment (9,   3)

bus *n*
groups of wires which carry signals between units in the CPU (7,   1)

byte *n*
group of bits which form one character, usually 1 byte = 8 bits (7,   4)

CAD *n*
Computer **A**ided **D**esign (2,   4)

card reader *n*
input device which reads information from special cards, e.g. punched cards (4,1)

catalogue *n*
list of the names and addresses of the files stored on the surface of a disc (6,   1)

cell *n*
individual storage area in the main memory (7,   3)

central processing unit *n*
the electronic 'brain' of the computer which mainly consists of the processor and the main memory (1,   1)

central processor *n*
see central processing unit (1,   4)

character *n*
letter, number, symbol or blank space produced by a keyboard (3,   1)

character printer *n*
printer which prints one character at a time (5,   1)

chief programmer *n*
person in charge of the applications and systems programmers (10,   3)

chip *n*
electronic device composed of a slice of silicon with thousands of electronic components and circuits engraved on it (7,   1)

clock *n*
part of the CU which sends regular pulses to all the other units in the computer system to keep them in step (7,   1)

COBOL *n*
COmmon **B**usiness **O**riented **L**anguage High-level language particularly suitable for business applications (9,   1)

colour monitor *n*
monitor which can display many different colours at the same time (5,   1)

COM *n*
Computer **O**utput on **M**icrofilm (5,   3)

communications satellite *n*
receiver/transmitter which orbits the Earth (8,   1)

compiler *n*
systems program used to translate a complete high-level language program into a machine code program (9,   3)

computer aided design *n*
design done using computer graphics (2,   4)

computer installation *n*
see mainframe computer (1,   1)

computer manager *n*
person in charge of a small computer installation who does the work of a data processing manager and an operations manager (10,   3)

computer operator *n*
person who controls and maintains the computer hardware (10,   3)

computer output on microfilm *n*
reduced images of documents stored on photographic film using a laser device (5,   3)

computerise *v*
put an existing system onto a computer (10,   3)

computerspeak *n*
slang word used to describe the speech produced by a speech synthesiser (5,   3)

control unit *n*
part of the processor which controls all the other parts of the computer system (7,   1)

CPU *n*
Central **P**rocessing **U**nit (1,   1)

create *v*
design the layout of database records (11,   3)

CU *n*
Control **U**nit (7,   1)

cursor *n*
symbol on a VDU screen which indicates where the next character will be displayed (2,   1)

cursor control device *n*
input device used to move cursor around a VDU screen (4,   1)

custom program *n*
a program written to perform a particular function in a particular situation (10,   1)

DAC *n*
Digital to **A**nalogue **C**onverter (5,   1)

daisywheel printer *n*
character impact printer which has solid characters positioned around a wheel (5,   1)

data *n*
particular information to be processed, e.g. names, numbers etc. (1,   1)

data communications system *n*

computer system connected by telecommunications links, e.g. telephone lines (8,   1)

data control clerk *n*
person who checks data handed in to the data preparation department and returns it to the owner when the job is complete (10,   3)

data controller *n*
person who supervises the data control clerks (10,   3)

data preparation supervisor *n*
person in charge of the data preparation department (10,   3)

data processing manager *n*
person in overall charge of a large computer installation (10,   3)

data slot *n*
circulating storage area in a LAN which can carry data around the network (8,   1)

database *n*
large collection of related information (11,   3)

database management system *n*
set of systems programs which manages a database and enables the data to be used by various applications programs (10,   1)

database program *n*
applications program used for information retrieval which allows a large amount of data to be searched for a particular item (10,   1)

datacomm system *n*
see data communications system (8,   1)

DBMS *n*
Data**B**ase **M**anagement **S**ystem (10,   1)

debug *v*
find a mistake or fault and correct it (9,   3)

dedicated line *n*
telephone line which is permanently connected to a computer system (8,   1)

delete *v*
erase from the VDU screen or memory (11,   3)

dialled line *n*
telephone line which is only connected to a computer system when required (8,   1)

digital signal *n*
signal which changes in steps, i.e. is made up of discrete pulses (4,   1)

digital to analogue converter *n*
component which changes a digital signal into an analogue signal (5,   1)

direct access *adj*
see random access (6,   1)

directory *n*
see catalogue (6,   1)

disc *n*
magnetic storage medium in the form of a thin, flat, circular plate (6,   1)

disc drive *n*
storage device which spins disc and contains read/write head (6,   1)

disc pack *n*
set of hard discs on one spindle (6,   3)

discette *n*
small disc, i.e. floppy disc (6,   3)

disk *n*
American spelling of disc (6,   1)

distributed processing *n*
processing shared between a number of interconnected processors (7,   1)

document reader *n*
input device which can transfer information from a document to a computer directly (4,   3)

dot-matrix printer *n*
character impact printer which prints characters as a pattern of dots (5,   1)

download *v*
copy information from the memory of a large computer to the memory of a smaller computer (8,   3)

drum plotter *n*
plotter which has a drum over which the paper is placed (5,   5)

edit *v*
make changes and corrections (2,   1)

editor *n*
utility program which allows the user to make changes and corrections to a program (10,   1)

electronic mail *n*
datacomm service which allows messages to be exchanged between computers (8,   3)

embedded code *n*
special command code inserted into a text to control the way in which the text will be printed out (12,   1)

EPROM *n*
Eraseable **P**rogrammable **R**ead **O**nly **M**emory (7,   3)

exchangeable *adj*
can be removed and replaced by another unit (6,   3)

execute *v*
carry out the program instructions step by step (1,   1)

external memory *n*
storage area outside of the CPU, i.e. backing store (1,   4)

facsimile machine *n*
terminal which enables images

of original documents to be transmitted and received (8, 3)

fast printer *n*
printer which prints a line or a page at a time (5, 1)

fax service *n*
facsimile machine service (8, 3)

fibre optics cable *n*
cable made from thin strands of glass, used to carry signals in the form of light beams (8, 1)

field *n*
single group of information in a record (11, 3)

file *n*
collection of records (11, 3)

file *n*
section of information stored in a backing store (6, 1)

file librarian *n*
person who looks after the files and keeps them up to date (10, 3)

flatbed plotter *n*
plotter which has a flat board on which the paper is placed (5, 5)

floppy disc *n*
small, flexible magnetic disc used as a storage medium (6, 3)

flowchart *n*
diagram used to show steps in a process and to design a computer program (9, 4)

format *v*
design position or layout of something, e.g. mark tracks and sectors on the surface of a disc (6, 1)

FORTRAN *n*
FORmula **TRAN**slator High-level language particularly suitable for scientific and engineering applications (9, 1)

graphics program *n*
applications program which displays statistical data in the form of graphs (12, 1)

graphics tablet *n*
input device used for copying drawings by tracing over them with a special pen (4, 1)

graphics terminal *n*
terminal which is used for CAD and has a high resolution VDU screen, keyboard and lightpen (8, 1)

hard disc *n*
solid magnetic disc used as a storage medium (6, 3)

hardcopy printout *n*
computer output printed on paper (5, 1)

hardware *n*
pieces of equipment making up a computer system (1, 1)

high resolution display *n*
VDU screen display made up of small pixels giving very detailed graphics (5, 1)

high-level language *n*
computer language in which each instruction translates into many machine code instructions (9, 1)

housekeeping routine *n*
common task performed by a utility program, e.g. copying a file from tape to disc (10, 1)

icon *n*
symbol displayed on VDU screen to represent a process that can be carried out by a program (4, 1)

Id. *n*
identification number used to access a computer system (2, 4)

immediate access memory *n*
memory which can be accessed with almost no delay, i.e. the main memory (7, 3)

impact printer *n*
printer which operates by forcing a printhead into contact with an inked ribbon and paper (5, 1)

ink-jet printer *n*
printer which operates by spraying quick-drying ink onto paper (5, 1)

input *n*
information fed into a computer (1, 1)

input *v*
enter information into the CPU (1, 1)

input device *n*
piece of equipment which allows information to be fed into a computer in a form that can be understood by the CPU, e.g. keyboard (1, 1)

integrated package *n*
set of applications programs which can all access the same data (10, 1)

intelligent terminal *n*
terminal which has its own internal processor (8, 1)

interactive *adj*
responds to data which is input while the program is being executed (9, 1)

internal memory *n*
storage area inside the CPU, i.e. the main memory (7, 3)

interpreter *n*
systems program used to translate a high-level language program into machine code, line by line, each time the high-level program is run (9, 3)

joystick *n*
cursor control input device with a vertical lever, used to move cursor quickly around screen (4, 1)

justification *n*
alignment of the edges of a text (12, 1)

K *adj*
kilobyte = 2^{10} = 1024 bytes (7, 4)

key *n*
data in the key field of a record (11, 3)

key field *n*
field which identifies a record uniquely (11, 3)

key station *n*
offline unit for preparation of data. Data keyed in using the keyboard is stored on disc or tape (4, 1)

key-to-disc-system *n*
offline system for transferring keyboard input to magnetic disc (4, 1)

key-to-tape system *n*
offline system for transferring keyboard input to magnetic tape (4, 1)

keyboard *n*
input device consisting of a large number of keys which emit coded electrical pulses when pressed (1, 1)

keyboard operator *n*
person who keys information into a key station (10, 3)

keypunch *n*
offline keyboard device which punches holes in punched cards in response to input from the keyboard (4, 1)

LAN *n*
Local Area Network (8, 1)

language translator *n*
systems program which translates computer languages into machine code, i.e. assembler, compiler or interpreter (10, 1)

laser printer *n*
printer which operates using laser light to photocopy documents (5, 1)

lightpen *n*
pen-shaped input device which operates by sensing light. Can be used to 'draw' on VDU screen (4, 1)

line printer *n*
printer which prints a line at a time (5, 1)

LISP *n*
LISt **P**rocessing High-level language used for artificial intelligence research (9, 1)

list *v*
display program instructions line by line (2, 3)

load *v*
copy program from backing store to main memory (2, 3)

local area network *n*
computers connected together
within a small area (8, 1)

location *n*
see cell (7, 3)

log *n*
a record, kept by a computer in a
multi-user system, of information
such as when, for how long and by
whom the CPU was used (2, 1)

log in *v adv*
begin log of access to the CPU
(2, 1)

log out *v adv*
end log of access to the CPU
(2, 1)

logging procedure *n*
steps which have to be followed
to log in or log out (2, 1)

LOGO *n*
high-level language used to
control small robot called a 'turtle'
(9, 1)

loop network *n*
network which has all its devices
connected in a ring (8, 1)

low resolution display *n*
VDU screen display made up of
large pixels giving crude graphics
(5, 1)

low-level language *n*
computer language in which
one instruction is required for each
operation (9, 1)

LQ *adj*
Letter Quality, i.e. good enough
to be used for business letters
(5, 1)

machine code *n*
binary code numbers which can
be directly understood by the CPU
(9, 1)

magnetic disc *n*
see disc (1, 1)

**magnetic ink character
reader** *n*
document reader input device
which can read characters printed
with magnetic ink (4, 3)

**magnetic ink character
recognition** *n*
reading of characters printed
with magnetic ink to provide direct
input for a computer (4, 3)

magnetic tape *n*
see tape (6, 1)

mail merging *n*
combining a database with a
word processor text to personalise
standard letters (11, 1)

mailbox *n*
part of a computer's memory
used for storing messages in an
electronic mail system (8, 3)

main memory *n*
storage area in the CPU which
holds the programs and data
currently being used (1, 1)

main store *n*
see main memory (1, 4)

mainframe *n*
common abbreviation for
mainframe computer (1, 1)

mainframe computer *n*
largest and most powerful type
of computer (1, 1)

Mb *n*
megabyte = 2^{20} bytes (7, 3)

memory address *n*
code number giving the position
of a cell in memory (7, 3)

merge *v*
combine two or more files to
make one larger file (11, 3)

message switching service *n*
datacomm service which
enables messages to be sent
between computers or terminals
(8, 3)

MICR *n*
Magnetic **I**nk **C**haracter
Recognition (4, 3)

micro *n*
common abbreviation for
microcomputer (1, 1)

microcomputer *n*
smallest and least powerful type
of computer (1, 1)

microfilm *n*
photographic film used as an
output medium for storing images
of documents in a reduced form
(5, 3)

microwave radio *n*
high frequency radio which uses
dish aerials for data
communications (8, 1)

mini *n*
common abbreviation for
minicomputer (1, 1)

minicomputer *n*
type of computer which is
smaller than a mainframe
computer but larger than a
microcomputer (1, 1)

mnemonic *n*
abbreviation used to make
words easy to remember (9, 1)

modem *n*
a modulator/demodulator
connected between a computer
and a telephone line which
converts signals to the correct
form, i.e. analogue or digital
(8, 1)

monitor *n*
specially adapted television
which gives a good quality display
of computer output (1, 1)

monochrome monitor *n*
monitor which can only display
one colour at a time, usually green
or amber (5, 1)

mouse *n*
small, box-shaped, cursor
control input device with a ball
underneath allowing it to be rolled
across the top of a desk (4, 1)

multi-user configuration *n*
a number of terminals sharing
one computer (1, 3)

multiplexer *n*
electronic device which allows
many terminals to share the same
equipment (1, 3)

network configuration *n*
a number of computers
connected together and able to
communicate with each other
(1, 3)

NLQ *adj*
Near **L**etter **Q**uality, i.e. better
than the normal dot-matrix print
(5, 1)

non-exchangeable *adj*
cannot be removed and replaced
by another unit (6, 3)

non-impact printer *n*
printer which prints characters
without forcing a printhead into
contact with paper (5, 1)

numeric keypad *n*
small keyboard with keys
arranged like a calculator, used to
simplify the input of numerical
data (4, 1)

OCR *n*
Optical **C**haracter **R**ecognition
(4, 3)

offline *adj*
not directly connected to or
controlled by the CPU (4, 1)

OMR *n*
Optical **M**ark **R**ecognition
(4, 3)

online *adj*
directly connected to and
controlled by the CPU (4, 1)

operating system *n*
group of systems programs
which manage and co-ordinate all
the software and hardware of a
computer system (10, 1)

operations manager *n*
person in charge of the day-to-
day running of the data processing
operations (10, 3)

optical character reader *n*
document reader input device
which reads characters directly by
sensing reflection of light (4, 3)

optical character recognition
n
reading of special characters
using the reflection of light to
provide direct input for a computer
(4, 3)

optical mark reader *n*
document reader input device
which reads marks on documents
by sensing reflection of light
(4, 3)

optical mark recognition *n*
reading of special marks using
the reflection of light to provide
direct input for a computer (4, 3)

output *v*
bring information out of a computer (1,   1)

output *n*
information brought out of a computer (1,   1)

output device *n*
piece of equipment which displays the results of processing in a form which can be understood by humans (1,   1)

PASCAL *n*
high-level language popular in colleges and universities (9,   1)

password *n*
secret word which must be input before access is given to a computer system (2,   1)

payroll program *n*
applications program used for calculating salaries (10,   1)

PC *n*
Personal Computer (1,   3)

peripheral *n*
device connected to and controlled by the CPU, including input devices output devices and storage devices (1,   1)

personal computer *n*
another name for a microcomputer (1,   3)

pixel *n*
PICTure ELement (5,   1)

plotter *n*
output device used for printing detailed drawings (5,   5)

primary store *n*
see main memory (1,   4)

printer *n*
output device used for printing text and graphics on paper (1,   1)

process *v*
manipulate and carry out operations on data (1,   1)

processor *n*
part of a computer which does all the processing and controls all the other devices in the computer system, sometimes referred to as the CPU (1,   1)

program *n*
set of instructions telling the computer what to do (1,   1)

program counter *n*
register in the CU used to hold the address of the next instruction to be carried out (7,   1)

program library *n*
group of applications programs stored in a backing store and readily available to users (10,   1)

programmer *n*
person who writes and modifies programs (10,   3)

PROM *n*
Programmable Read Only Memory (7,   3)

prompt *n*
words or symbols displayed on VDU screen indicating that the computer is ready for keyboard input (2,   1)

punched card *n*
input medium consisting of a piece of thin cardboard with holes punched in it according to a special code, to represent the computer input (4,   1)

QUIT *v*
command used to come out of BASIC language (2,   1)

QWERTY keyboard *n*
keyboard with alphanumeric keys in the standard arrangement, i.e. with Q,W,E,R,T,Y as the first six letters (3,   1)

RAM *n*
Random Access Memory (7,   3)

random access *adj*
information can be written to or read from each part with equal speed and ease (6,   1)

random access memory *n*
storage area which allows a computer to write information to it and read information from it (7,   3)

read only memory *n*
storage area which allows a computer to read information from it but does not allow the computer to write information to it (7,   3)

read/write head *n*
component which reads and writes magnetic marks (6,   1)

record *n*
unit of a file which is made up of a number of related fields of information (11,   3)

register *n*
small, short-term memory used for a special purpose, e.g. accumulator, program counter (7,   1)

remote access terminal *n*
terminal which is a long distance away from a central computer (8,   1)

ROM *n*
Read Only Memory (7,   3)

run *v*
execute a program line by line (1,   1)

save *v*
copy a program from the main memory to a backing store (2,   3)

screen *n*
display area of a monitor (1,   4)

screen dump *n*
VDU screen display copied to a printer (10,   1)

screen mode *n*
computer setting which determines the way in which the computer will display text and graphics on a VDU screen (5,   1)

scroll *v*
move the whole display up, down or across the VDU screen (12,   3)

search *v*
look for particular data (11,   3)

secondary store *n*
see backing store (1,   4)

sector *n*
subdivision of a track on disc surface (6,   1)

shift leader *n*
chief computer operator (10,   3)

signing-on message *n*
words which appear on monitor screen when computer is first switched on giving details of computer system (2,   1)

single cable network *n*
network which has all its devices connected to one cable (8,   1)

single-sided disc *n*
disc which can only be formatted on one surface (6,   1)

slow printer *n*
printer which cannot print any more than one character at a time (5,   1)

software *n*
computer information including programs and data (1,   1)

sort *v*
put into alphabetical or numerical order (11,   3)

speech synthesis *n*
artificial speaking achieved by combining various stored sound patterns (5,   3)

spelling checker *n*
computer program used with a word processor which checks the spelling in a text (12,   1)

spreadsheet program *n*
type of program used for financial planning (10,   1)

stand-alone configuration *n*
arrangement in which a computer and its peripherals are not connected to any other computer system (1,   3)

storage device *n*
piece of equipment which allows information to be stored permanently. Usually operates using magnetism, e.g. disc drive (1,   1)

storage medium *n*
material used for storing information, e.g. magnetic tape (1,   1)

system configuration *n*
way in which a computer system is connected together (1,   3)

systems analyst *n*
person who studies existing systems to advise on putting them on to a computer. He or she is also responsible for designing the new computerised system and for getting it into operation (10,   3)

systems program *n*
program which controls a basic function of a computer system (10, 1)

systems programmer *n*
person who writes and modifies systems programs (10, 3)

tape *n*
magnetic storage medium like audio tape (6, 5)

teletext service *n*
videotex information service which broadcasts a database along with television signals. It only allows transfer of information in one direction (8, 3)

teletype terminal *n*
terminal consisting of a keyboard and a printer (8, 1)

telex *n*
message switching datacomm system which uses teleprinters (8, 3)

terminal *n*
unit made up of at least one input and one output device (8, 1)

thermal printer *n*
printer which forms characters by heating heat-sensitive paper (5, 1)

time-sharing *adj*
system whereby each terminal is connected to the central processor in turn, for a fraction of a second (1, 3)

touchpad *n*
input device which only has to be touched to input data (4, 1)

track *n*
circular storage area marked on the surface of a disc (6, 1)

trackerball *n*
cursor control input device which moves the cursor in relation to the rotation of a ball (4, 1)

update *v*
change data to include new information (11, 3)

user *n*
person who operates a small computer system or terminal (1, 3)

user-friendly *adj*
easy to use, giving helpful messages to indicate to the user what is happening (9, 1)

utility program *n*
small systems program which performs one simple task, e.g. housekeeping routine (10, 1)

VDU *n*
Visual **D**isplay **U**nit (1, 1)

VDU terminal *n*
input/output unit connected to a mainframe computer, consisting of a monitor screen and a keyboard (8, 1)

verify *v*
check for errors (6, 1)

video disc *n*
storage medium similar to a magnetic disc but has information written onto it by a laser (6, 1)

videotex service *n*
datacomm information service which allows large amounts of information to be transmitted and displayed on television or VDU screens (8, 3)

viewdata service *n*
videotex information service which uses telephone lines to transmit information in both directions (8, 3)

visual display unit *n*
output device which displays computer output on a screen (1, 1)

voice output *n*
output in a form similar to human speech (5, 3)

voice recognition device *n*
input device which accepts input in the form of human speech (4, 1)

volatile *adj*
does not hold data when switched off (6, 1)

WAN *n*
Wide **A**rea **N**etwork (8, 1)

wide area network *n*
network connected over a large area (8, 1)

wildcard character *n*
special symbol used in database programs to represent any combination of characters (11, 3)

Winchester *n*
small hard disc drive used with microcomputers (6, 3)

Winchester disc *n*
small hard disc used with microcomputers (6, 1)

word processor program *n*
applications program used for text manipulation (10, 1)

word-wrap *n*
facility which automatically moves a word to the next line if there is not enough space for the complete word on the current line (12, 1)

working memory *n*
see main memory (7, 3)

WYSIWYG *adj*
What **Y**ou **S**ee **I**s **W**hat **Y**ou **G**et
Used to describe word processor programs which always display text exactly as it will be printed out (12, 1)

2 Quiz

Unit 1
1 What is the largest type of computer?
2 What are microcomputers commonly called?
3 What term is used for a set of instructions telling the computer what to do?
4 What is the CPU?
5 What name is given to devices connected to the CPU?
6 What is a VDU?
7 What is the most common input device?
8 Magnetic tape and magnetic disc are two types of .... media.
9 What part of the CPU stores programs and data?
0 What system

configuration allows a number of computers to be connected together?

Unit 2
1 What name is given to the symbol which indicates that the computer is ready to accept input from the keyboard?
2 What name is given to the symbol which shows where the next input will be displayed?
3 What key must be pressed before the input can be processed or stored in the main memory?
4 A secret .... is used to limit access to a computer system.
5 Which computer language is

found on most microcomputers?
6 What name is given to the record of when a terminal enters and leaves a computer system?
7 What BASIC command is used to copy a program from a storage medium to the main memory?
8 What BASIC command is used to start the execution of a program?
9 What BASIC command is used to display a program line by line on a VDU screen?
10 What BASIC command is used to copy a program from the main memory to a backing store?

Unit 3

1 What name is given to the standard alphanumeric keyboard layout?
2 What is the general term for letters, numbers, symbols and blank spaces?
3 What word means that if a key is held down its function will be repeated again and again?
4 Which function produces a mixture of upper-case and lower-case characters?
5 Which key is used to stop a program without losing the program from memory?
6 What name is given to the # symbol?
7 What name is given to the & symbol?
8 What name is given to the ' symbol?
9 What name is given to the \ symbol?
10 What name is given to the * symbol?

Unit 4

1 What word means 'not connected to or controlled by the CPU'?
2 What device is used to transfer keyboard input onto punched cards?
3 What input device allows numerical data to be input easily?
4 What cursor control device is operated by rolling it across a desk top?
5 What cursor control device is used for fast action games?
6 What input devices can be used to 'draw' directly onto a VDU screen?
7 What is CAD?
8 What input device can be used for copying detailed drawings?
9 What is OCR?
10 What name is given to the black and white parallel lines used to identify items?

Unit 5

1 What name is given to a specially adapted television which can only display one colour?
2 What is the common name for picture elements?
3 What type of display gives very detailed graphics?
4 What is the output from a printer known as?
5 Which type of printer has characters positioned around a wheel?
6 Which type of printer prints characters as a pattern of dots?
7 What is NLQ?
8 What is COM?
9 What is a DAC?
10 What output device is used to print detailed drawings?

Unit 6

1 What term is used for a group of information stored in a backing store?
2 What term is used for the time taken to find and transfer a file from backing store?

3 What name is given to the circular storage areas on the surface of a magnetic disc?
4 What are the subdivisions of tracks called?
5 What storage device is used to spin a magnetic disc?
6 To .... a disc is to mark tracks and sectors on its surface.
7 What name is given to the list of file names and addresses on a magnetic disc?
8 A number of hard discs stacked together on one spindle form a ....
9 What storage device uses a small hard disc?
10 What name is given to flexible magnetic discs?

Unit 7

1 The main components of the CPU are the main memory and the ....
2 What is the ALU?
3 Which register in the ALU is used to temporarily hold the data item currently being processed?
4 Which component of the CU sends out regular pulses to each unit to keep them in step?
5 What is the term used for the storage locations in the main memory?
6 What is RAM?
7 What is ROM?
8 What is the common name for a binary digit?
9 Which international code is commonly used to represent characters by an 8 bit binary number?
10 What is the term used for the number of bits which make up one character, i.e. 8 bits?

Unit 8

1 Which type of terminal is made up of a keyboard and a printer?
2 What is a LAN?
3 What device is used to connect a computer to a telephone line?
4 Which type of modem has rubber cups into which an ordinary telephone can be plugged?
5 Which type of cable allows data to be transmitted as pulses of light?
6 What unit is used to measure the rate of data transmission?
7 What is the common name for the Teleprinter Exchange service?
8 Which type of videotex system broadcasts data along with ordinary television signals?
9 Which type of videotex system uses telephone lines to provide two-way communications?
10 What term is used for the process of copying programs from a large central computer into a smaller computer?

Unit 9

1 What is the only type of language that computers can understand directly?

2 Which type of lowlevel language uses mnemonics?
3 What special type of program translates assembly language into machine code?
4 What word means 'able to respond to data which is input while the program is running'?
5 What term is used for a computer language in which each instruction translates into many machine code instructions?
6 Which high-level language is particularly suited to solving problems using formulas in science and engineering?
7 What do the letters COBOL stand for?
8 What type of diagram is used to show the sequence of a computer program?
9 What special type of program translates highlevel programs into machine codes line by line?
10 What special type of program translates complete highlevel programs into machine code programs?

Unit 10

1 What is the general term for information used in computer systems?
2 What type of programs are designed for particular situations and are often written by the user?
3 What type of applications program is used for information retrieval?
4 What type of applications program is used for financial planning?
5 A set of applications programs which can share the same data is known as an ....
6 Which type of programs control the basic functions of a computer?
7 What name is given to the set of programs which manages and co-ordinates all the hardware and software?
8 What is a DBMS?
9 Which person studies existing systems and advises on the feasibility of computerising them?
10 What is the title of the person in overall charge of a large computer system?

Unit 11

1 Which type of impact printer can be used to print graphs?
2 Which type of impact printer is used for printing business letters?
3 Which type of applications program is used for drawing graphs?
4 What word means 'edit by adding new information'?
5 What is the name given to a large collection of related information?
6 What name is given to a group of records in a database?

7 Each type of information on a database record is known as a ....

8 What is the name given to a field used to uniquely identify a record?

9 Symbols used to represent any letter or number of letters are known as ....

10 To .... files means 'to combine two or more files to make a larger file'.

Unit 12

1 Which type of applications program is used for the creation and manipulation of texts?

2 What do the letters WYSIWYG stand for?

3 Which facility automatically moves a word to a new line if there is not enough space on the current line?

4 What is the name given to special characters inserted into a text to control the way in which the text will be printed out?

5 What type of special program is used with a word processor to indicate if any word has been incorrectly spelled?

6 Which word processor facility lines up the edges of a text?

7 Which facility enables names and addresses from a database to be automatically inserted into a standard text?

8 Which type of applications program displays data in an array?

9 The boxes formed by the intersection of rows and columns in a spreadsheet are known as ....

10 .... means 'moving a complete display horizontally or vertically on a VDU screen'.

3 Tapescripts

Tapescript 1: Computer system configurations

There are three main ways of connecting the devices in a computer system.

One method results in what is known as a **stand-alone configuration**. In this arrangement each computer is separate, i.e. it is not connected to any other computer. Each computer, with its peripherals, forms a complete system by itself and can be operated by one person, known as the **user**. Microcomputers, sometimes referred to as **personal computers** or **PCs**, are often used in a stand-alone configuration.

A second method of connection results in what is known as a **network configuration**. In this arrangement many computers are connected together and can communicate with each other, sometimes over long distances. This allows them to exchange data and to share the same peripherals. In this way, each user can quickly access large amounts of data and the cost of equipment can be kept to a minimum.

The last method of connection results in what is known as a **multi-user configuration**. In this arrangement many people can use the same computer. Each user operates a **VDU terminal** which consists of a **VDU** screen and a keyboard. Each terminal is connected in turn to the CPU for a fraction of a second. This **time-sharing** of the CPU is controlled by a device called a **multiplexer**. The time-sharing happens so quickly that it seems as if all the terminals are using the CPU at once. A multi-user configuration is often used with mainframe computers.

Tapescript 2: BASIC commands

When access has been gained to the system and a language has been chosen, the user can issue commands or key in new programs using the keyboard. The input must follow the rules of the chosen language. Some languages, e.g. BASIC, cause **error messages** such as 'Mistake' or 'Syntax at line 30', to be displayed on the monitor screen if the rules of the language are not followed.

By issuing commands, various functions can be controlled. For example, using the language BASIC, a program can be copied from a storage medium to the main memory by the command **load**. The user keys in **l-o-a-d** followed by the name of the required program, inside quotation marks. When the RETURN key is pressed, the program of that name will be loaded into the main memory.

The program in the main memory can be listed on the screen, line by line, by the command **list**. In this case the user has only to key in **l-i-s-t** and press the RETURN key.

Similarly, the command **run** will start the execution of the program in the main memory. The user keys in **r-u-n** and presses the RETURN key.

A new program can be copied from the main memory to a storage medium by the command **save**. In this case, the user must first choose a name for the new program and then key in **s-a-v-e** followed by the chosen name, inside quotation marks. When the RETURN key is pressed the new program will be saved to the storage medium.

Many other commands can be used to control the peripherals and perform other functions.

Tapescript 3: Keyboard variations

Here is another computer keyboard. It is similar to the first one but there are a number of differences.

The most obvious difference is that there are more keys on this keyboard. There is a numeric keypad to the right of the main alphanumeric keyboard. This makes it easier to input a lot of numerical data.

Next to the numeric keypad are extra editing keys. These are called: HOME, CLEAR, LINE INSERT CHARACTER, LINE DELETE CHARACTER and SCROLL.

Along the top of the main keyboard there are extra function keys. These are called: HELP, UNDO, REPEAT, CALCULATE, PRINT, INTERRUPT, MENU and FINISH.

There is also an extra key called STOP on the bottom row of the keyboard, to the right of the SPACE BAR.

There are, however, a few keys which do not appear on this keyboard. These are BREAK, COPY and SHIFT LOCK. There are also two symbols which do not appear.

Some of the function keys have different labels, e.g. ESCAPE is labelled E-S-C and C-T-R-L is labelled CONTROL. The RETURN key, the TAB key and the DELETE key have arrow labels instead of words.

The positions of some of the keys are also different. On this keyboard, the ESCAPE and CONTROL keys are on the bottom row, the ARROW keys are also lower down and the DELETE key is directly above the RETURN key.

Although the alphanumeric keys have the same **QWERTY** layout as before, most of the symbols have different positions. Notice, for example, on this keyboard, the number 0 key has an upper-case symbol.

Lastly, the user-defined function keys on this keyboard are in a different position, on the top right of the keyboard. They are in the form of a microscreen. This consists of special touch-sensitive keys which display the names of the defined functions, as the program is running.

Tapescript 4: Document readers

It is often necessary to transfer information from documents to a computer. This may take a long time using a keyboard and it is easy to make mistakes and introduce errors as the information is being keyed in. However, it is possible for computers to read documents directly using **document reader** devices.

There are various different types of document readers. **Optical** devices use the reflection of light to sense marks or characters on the document. For example, an **optical mark reader** can read lines drawn at fixed positions on specially prepared forms. Forms of this kind are often used for questionnaires and multiple-choice examination papers. However, they are sometimes difficult to fill in or understand. This method of reading documents is known as **OMR** (**O**ptical **M**ark **R**ecognition).

A **bar code reader**, on the other hand, reads specially printed patterns of black and white parallel lines of varying thickness. These line patterns are called **bar codes** and represent numbers which are used to identify items. For example, packets and tins of food often have bar codes printed on them as do some library books.

Other types of document readers are able to read characters by comparing them with shape patterns stored in the main memory. These devices can usually only recognise one or two special styles of characters.

An **optical character reader** can read characters printed with printer's ink or, sometimes, handwritten characters, if these are written very carefully in a special style. Optical characters are sometimes used on domestic bills, e.g. electricity bills. We call this method of reading documents **OCR** (**O**ptical **C**haracter **R**ecognition).

A **magnetic ink character reader** reads characters printed with special magnetic ink. These characters are formed from a series of thin vertical bars. They are used for account numbers and sorting codes on bank cheques since magnetic ink characters are more difficult to forge and can still be read even when folded or written on. This method is called **MICR** (**M**agnetic **I**nk **C**haracter **R**ecognition).

Tapescript 5: Forms of output

Instead of printing the output from a computer onto paper, it can be put onto special photographic film called **microfilm**.

This is done using a laser output device which scans the photographic film and produces images of the text which are a fraction of their original size. In this way, microfilm can be used to store large amounts of text in a very compact form, for long periods, without deterioration. This is very useful for keeping such things as large numbers of historical records without taking up too much space.

However, one problem with **computer output** on **microfilm** is that the computer is not able to read and display the microfilm text directly. To allow the user to see the text, a special microfilm reader device must be used. This finds the required page on the film, then magnifies and displays it on a screen.

Computer output can also be used for machine control. By passing the output through a component called a **DAC** (a **D**igital to **A**nalogue **C**onverter), the computer can control the movement of mechanical devices such as robots and machine tools. These computer controlled machines are used in industry for the production and assembly of mechanical parts, for example. in the production of motor cars.

Another form of computer output which may be important in the future is **voice output**. Listen to this example of voice output from a computer:

[HELLO! THIS IS AN EXAMPLE OF A COMPUTER SPEAKING USING SPEECH SYNTHESIS]

As you heard, the computer does not sound exactly like a human being but produces what is known as '**computerspeak**'.

Too much memory would be required to store every possible word as well as all the features of human speech such as intonation. Instead, the basic sound patterns which make up speech are stored. The computer can then be programmed to put these basic sounds together in different combinations to produce speech. This process is known as **speech synthesis**.

Voice output is particularly useful for people who are not able to use a VDU screen. For example, a blind person or someone who is driving a vehicle. As speech synthesis is improved, it may, in the future, be used for translation and language teaching.

Tapescript 6: Types of discs

There are two types of discs, **hard discs** and **floppy discs**.

Hard discs are made of metal and are about 10 inches in diameter with about 200 tracks on each surface. Usually, a number of hard discs are stacked together on one spindle to form a **disc pack**.

Some disc packs are **exchangeable**, i.e. one disc pack can be removed from the disc drive and be replaced by another one. They have moving heads which move across the surface of the discs to the required track.

Other disc packs are **non-exchangeable**, being sealed inside a container along with the disc drive. They have a separate head fixed over each track, giving them a much faster access time. However, they are much more expensive than moving head disc packs.

Hard discs can hold large quantities of information, have very fast access times and are very reliable but they are quite expensive. They are, therefore, usually used with mainframe computers and minicomputers.

A **Winchester** storage device uses a small hard disc of about 3.5 inches in diameter, sealed in a container along with the disc drive. The disc is not exchangeable but can hold as much information as a larger disc because of the precision of the mechanism. Being small, reliable and relatively inexpensive, Winchesters are suitable for use with microcomputers.

The other type of disc is the **floppy disc** or **discette**. Being made of plastic, they are very flexible and are enclosed in a protective jacket. They come in a variety of sizes, e.g 5.25 inches, 3.5 inches and 3 inches in diameter. They usually have 40 or 80 tracks per surface. Floppy discs are exchangeable but only one disc is used at a time. They cannot hold as much information as hard discs and have slower access times. In addition, they have to be handled with care since they are easily corrupted by dust, moisture or magnetism. It is common practice, therefore, to make **backup copies** of important information on a second disc. Being small, cheap and fairly reliable, they are commonly used with microcomputers.

Tapescript 7: Main memory

Part 1

The main memory is composed of a number of electronic chips. Each memory chip has thousands of storage **locations** or **cells** organised in a rectangular array of rows and columns as shown in Figure 7.3.

Each cell, therefore, has a unique **memory address** given by its row number and column number. For example, in Figure 7.3, the cell at the intersection of column 2 and row 5 has a six bit binary address of 010101. [PAUSE] Now write down the six bit binary address of the cell at the intersection of column 1 and row 6. [LONG PAUSE] Now write down the address of the cell at the intersection of column 5 and row 2. [LONG PAUSE]

Using the address, information stored in any part of the main memory can be found almost immediately. The main memory is therefore sometimes referred to as the **immediate access memory**. It is also known as the **internal memory** or the **working memory** because it is inside the CPU and stores the program and data currently being used.

Part 2

There are two different sections in the main memory known as **RAM** and **ROM**. **RAM** (**R**andom **A**ccess **M**emory) is used for the temporary storage of the user's programs and data. It is called random access because information can be written to or read from any cell with equal speed and ease. However, when information is written to a cell in RAM, any information previously stored there is destroyed. Furthermore, when the computer is switched off, all the information stored in RAM is lost.

Permanent storage of information is provided by **ROM** (**R**ead **O**nly **M**emory). The information stored in ROM is not lost when the computer is switched off. However, as its name suggests, the computer can only read information stored in ROM but cannot put information into it. The information stored in ROM usually includes such things as the instructions necessary for the basic operation of the computer and the languages which the computer uses. ROM is normally programmed by the computer manufacturer and cannot be changed. However, programmable ROM chips (**PROM**s) can be used to allow the user to permanently store his own programs. This can be done only by using a special programming device. Eraseable PROMs (**EPROMS**) are also available. Programs stored on EPROMS can be removed using ultraviolet light; then the EPROM can be reprogrammed.

The capacity of the main memory can sometimes be increased by adding extra RAM chips. Similarly the facilities available on the computer can usually be extended

by 'plugging in' more ROMs, e.g. a language ROM can be added to make more languages available on the computer.

Tapescript 8:   Data communications services

Data communications systems make it possible for powerful information services to be provided on a national and international scale. One type of data communications service is known as **message switching** and allows the communication of business and personal messages.

A message switching service commonly used by business people is the **TEL**eprinter **EX**change service, commonly known as **TELEX**. This enables messages to be sent between teletype terminals which print out each message as it is received.

A similar service known as **fax** uses facsimile machines to transmit copies of original documents. **Facsimile machines** operate by scanning the document and sending a digitised image to the receiving machine which then prints out a copy of the document.

Another message switching service, known as **electronic mail**, enables users to connect their computers to large central computers using modems and telephone lines. They can input messages which are stored by the central computer in a part of its memory known as a **mailbox**. The users can search the mailbox to find any messages addressed to them. If a message is found it can be **downloaded**, i.e. copied into the memory of the user's computer.

A different type of data communications service, known as **videotex**, enables large amounts of information to be transmitted and displayed on television or VDU screens.

For example, **teletext** transmits pages of information from a central **database**, i.e. a collection of data which can be searched to find particular items. This information is broadcast along with ordinary television signals and is received and displayed by specially adapted televisions. The user can select pages for display using a small keypad console. Teletext, however, provides the transfer of information in only one direction.

A different type of videotex service, called **viewdata**, uses telephone lines to transmit information. The information can be received by computers and displayed on television screens. Viewdata services provide two-way communications and make possible such services as tele-

shopping or tele-banking where the user can carry out transactions in the comfort of his or her own home.

These are only a few of the possible data communications services which are likely to become increasingly important for the transfer of information throughout the world.

Tapescript 9:   Interpreters and compilers

Computers cannot understand high-level languages directly. Programs written in these languages must be translated into machine code before they can be used.

Some high-level languages, such as BASIC, can be translated by a special program called an **interpreter**. An interpreter translates the high-level program into machine code, line by line. This interpretation is done every time the high-level program is run.

Interpretation slows down the execution of the program but allows it to be interactive. For example, the program can stop and wait for data to be input at the keyboard before continuing. It also makes writing and debugging a program easier. (**Debugging** a program means finding any errors or **bugs** and correcting them). For example, if an error occurs when the program is being keyed in or executed, the interpreter causes helpful **error messages** to be displayed on the VDU screen.

Interpreters do not use a huge amount of memory, and are therefore used with microcomputers.

Some high-level languages are designed to be translated in a different way by a special program called a **compiler**. This requires the high-level program to be translated only once.

A compiler translates the complete high-level program into a machine code program when it is first run. The compiled machine code program is then stored in the main memory. After that, each time the program is run, it is the compiled machine code program that is used. The program therefore can be executed very quickly.

Compiling a program, however, uses up a lot of memory, since memory space is required to hold the original high-level program, the compiled machine code program and the compiler itself. Compilers are therefore used mostly with mainframe computers.

Tapescript 10:   Computer personnel

A small microcomputer system can

be operated by one person, referred to as the **user**. A large mainframe computer installation, however, may require a large staff of specialists. The number of staff employed depends on factors such as the type and amount of work being done and the size of the computer system.

The person in overall charge of a large system is called the **data processing manager**. He or she co-ordinates the system analysis, the programming, the computer operations and the data preparation.

The job of the **systems analysts** is to study existing systems and advise on the feasibility of **computerising** them, i.e. putting them onto a computer. They are also responsible for designing the new computerised system and getting it into operation. This may include considerations such as staff training and preparation of manuals.

The people who use computer languages to write and modify programs are known as **programmers**. They can be divided into two main kinds. **Applications programmers** deal with applications programs and may use high-level languages. **Systems programmers**, on the other hand, deal with systems programs and work with low-level languages. There may also be a **chief programmer** in charge of the programming department.

The day-to-day running of the data processing operations is controlled by the **operations manager**. He or she is in charge of the computer operators, the data preparation staff, the file librarian and the data control clerks.

Computer operators control and maintain the computer hardware. They run the programs and monitor the progress of each job. The chief operator is known as the **shift leader**.

The data preparation department is controlled by the **data preparation supervisor**. In this department, **keyboard operators** key in data using offline key stations.

The **file librarian** looks after the files and keeps them up to date, and the **data control clerks** check data handed in to the department and return it to the user when the job is complete. The data control clerks are supervised by the **data controller**.

This describes the staff of a large computer installation. In a smaller system, some of these duties may overlap. For example, the person in overall charge may do the work of the data processing manager and the operations manager. In this case, he would be called the **computer manager**.

Tapescript 11: Database program

Part 1

One of the main types of program that would be used in a doctors' surgery is a database program. It can be used to store and retrieve information of any kind. We can get a better idea of how it works by comparing it with the older, manual methods of storing information, e.g. using a card index file.

Information is stored in a card index file by writing it on **record** cards. Each type of information written on a record is known as a **field**. For example, a doctor may keep record cards of patients. Each record would have a number of fields giving the patient's name, address, age, etc. An example of a patient's record card is shown in Figure 11.1.

When the records are put together they form a patient's **file**. If the doctor had other files with information on drugs, repeat prescriptions, etc., they would together form a **database** of information, i.e. a large collection of related information.

If one particular field is used to uniquely identify each record, it is known as the **key field** and the data in this field is known as the record **key**. It is usual to order the file on the key field. For example, if the key field was the surname of the patient, the records would be stored in alphabetical order of the patients' names.

In this way, a large amount of information can be accessed by finding the appropriate record card.

Part 2

There are, however, some problems with using a manual filing system for storing information. Firstly, it requires a lot of storage space. Secondly, it is not always obvious in which order to store the records. Thirdly, it may take a long time to find a particular record. Fourthly, if a record is not returned to its correct position in the file after use, it may prove very difficult to find it again. Lastly, if the information on a record has to be changed, a new card may have to be written out. If this happened frequently it could be time-consuming and expensive.

A better method of storing information is to use a **database program** on a computer. This would allow the user to **create** files and store them in a backing store.

To begin with, the layout of the records would be designed on the VDU screen by the user. The user would decide how many fields to have on a record and would give a name to each field. Then the data would be entered into each field using the keyboard. The program could then display one record at a time on the screen.

The file could easily be **updated** by adding new records, **deleting** existing records or **editing** items within existing records.

A great advantage of a computer database is that the records can be automatically **sorted** into alphabetical or numerical order using any field.

Another advantage of a computer database is that it can automatically **search** for a particular record. If the user keyed in some information, the computer would search and find all the records that contain that information.

Searches can be made on more than one field at a time. For example, if the doctor wanted to know all the patients with heart problems over the age of 40, the program would search on the **name** field and the **age** field simultaneously. In this way it would find all the records which matched both these conditions.

A general group of patients' records could also be searched for by using **wildcard** characters. These are symbols which represent any letter or number. For example, if the doctor wanted to find all the patients whose name began with the letters MA, a search would be made on the **name** field for MA*. The * symbol being the wildcard symbol in this example. In this way searches could be made for very general or incomplete information.

An added advantage of a database program is that it is impossible for records to get into the wrong position or lost since they are not actually removed from the file when they are used.

It is possible to automatically **merge** two or more files to make a larger file. If the files were originally in alphabetical order, the new, merged file will still be in alphabetical order.

Of course, a printout can be made of any records or any fields in a file using a printer. The layout of the printout can also be designed by the user.

A database program is therefore very useful for information storage and retrieval. It enables large amounts of information to be stored in a small space and to be manipulated quickly and easily.

**Tapescript 12:
Spreadsheet programs**

Spreadsheet programs are used in business for financial planning. This type of program displays information in the form of a table or array. Each column of the array is labelled with a letter and each row is labelled with a number. A simple example is shown in Figure 12.1.

Where a column and row intersect is known as a **cell** and can be referred to by its letter and number, e.g. cell A1, cell A2, cell B3, etc.

The spreadsheet program allows the array to have a very large number of cells. Only a few of them can be displayed on the VDU screen at a time. A **scrolling** facility is therefore provided which moves the display across or up and down the array, allowing the user to see any one group of cells.

Titles, values or formulas can be keyed into each cell. For example,

in Figure 12.1 the titles 'cost per item' and 'number of items' have been keyed into cells A1 and B1 respectively. Cell C1 should have the title 'total cost' keyed into it.

Also in this example, the values '0.65' and '100' have been keyed into cells A2 and B2 respectively. When the formula 'A2 multiplied by B2' is keyed into cell C2, the spreadsheet program automatically calculates and displays the result '65.00' in cell C2.

Similarly, when values are keyed into cells A3, A4, B3, B4 and the correct formulas are keyed into cells C3 and C4, the values of cells C3 and C4 are automatically calculated and displayed.

In this example, any value in column C can be automatically calculated by multiplying column A by column B.

Different formulas can be written into other cells in the array to automatically calculate such things

as tax on an item, discount for large orders, postage and packing charges, etc.

The main feature of this type of program is that, when the value in any one cell is changed, the program automatically recalculates and displays the correct values in all the other cells.

In this way, business managers can see how costs would be affected by a change in value of any one item. By experimenting to see the effects of different changes, they can make estimates and set prices for the future of their business.

Some spreadsheet programs have a **graphics** facility which displays spreadsheet values in the form of graphs, e.g. histograms, line graphs or pie charts. The spreadsheet and graphs can be stored in a backing store or printed out using a printer.

Spreadsheets are therefore very useful for financial planning and estimating because they allow the effects of changes in costs to be seen quickly and easily.

4 Key to the exercises

UNIT ONE
Task 1c microcomputer

Task 2
Mainframe *size* room, *power* +++, *use* in universities and government departments
Minicomputer *size* desk, *power* ++, *use* in banks and offices
Microcomputer *size* typewriter, *power* +, *use* at home, in education

Task 3 Student A
A program is a set of instructions which tell the computer what operations and processes have to be carried out and in what order.
1 The main memory stores the programs and data being used by the processor.
2 An input device is a peripheral which allows information to be fed into a computer.
3 A storage device is a peripheral used for the permanent storage of information.
Student B
Data is the particular information that has to be processed by a computer.
1 The processor is the brain of the computer. It does all the processing and controls all the other devices in the system.
2 An output device is a peripheral which allows information to be brought out of the computer.
3 A monitor is a specially adapted television commonly used as an output device.

Task 4 Problem 1
1e, 2d, 3a, 4b, 5c.

Problem 2
1d, 2/3e, 3/2a, 4c, 5b

Task 5
1 A computer (20), 2 information (20), 3 operations and processes (23), 4 The processor (42), 5 The main memory (44), 6 peripherals (49), 7 a printer (58), 8 A storage device (59).

Task 6 (Examples)
1 The mainframe is larger than the minicomputer.
2 The minicomputer is smaller than the mainframe.
3 The mainframe is more powerful than the minicomputer.
4 The minicomputer is less powerful than the mainframe.
5 The mainframe is used in universities and government departments but the minicomputer is used in banks and offices.

Task 7
12 The microcomputer has the smallest memory.
14 The mainframe is the most expensive.
15 The minicomputer has a larger memory than the microcomputer.
18 The microcomputer is less expensive than the minicomputer.

Task 8
1 multi-user, 2 network, 3 stand-alone

Task 9
1b, 2a, 3d, 4b, 5d, 6c, 7b, 8d, 9c.

Task 10
The mainframe is the biggest and most powerful. It is the size of a room and has the biggest memory. It is used in universities and government departments.
  The minicomputer is smaller than a mainframe but is bigger than a microcomputer. It is the size of a desk and is used in banks and offices.
  The microcomputer is the smallest. It is the size of a typewriter. It is the least powerful and is used at home and in education and business.

UNIT TWO
Task 1
1 A square or flashing light which indicates where the next input will appear on the screen.
2 By using a password which has to be keyed in before access is given.

Task 3
The actions are in this sequence :
5, 3, 1, 6, 4, 2.

Task 4
1 the computer system (2)
2 the password (16)
3 the system (30)
4 the log (27)
5 the correct password (39)

Task 5
2 LOGIN is typed and RETURN is pressed.

3 Your identification number is input.
4 The correct password is input.
5 A language is selected.
6 QUIT is typed and RETURN pressed.
7 LOGOUT is typed and RETURN pressed.
8 The terminal is switched off.

Task 7
1 LOAD, **2** LIST, **3** RUN, **4** SAVE

Task 8
1 Central Processing Unit
2 Visual Display Unit
3 Personal Computer
4 minicomputer
5 microcomputer
6 identification number

Task 9
1 Optical Character Recognition
2 American Standard Code for Information Interchange
3 Local Area Network
4 Near Letter Quality
5 Computer Aided Design

Task 10
1c, **2**e, **3**a, **4**b, **5**d.

Task 11
Before using a mainframe computer terminal, the user must log in. First, the terminal is switched on. When it is switched on, an arrow cursor appears on the screen. Next LOGIN is typed and RETURN pressed. When this is done, the computer displays a prompt asking for an identification number. Then your identification number is input. When this is input, another prompt is displayed asking for a password. After that, the correct password is input. When this is done, the computer indicates that the terminal has access to the system. Finally, a language is selected. When this is done, the computer accepts input in that language.

UNIT THREE
Task 1
1 Both have QWERTY keyboards which may be auto-repeating.
2 Computer keyboards have extra characters and keys which have special uses.

Task 2
1 User-defined function keys,
2 BREAK, **3** ESCAPE, **4** Editing keys (including COPY), **5** CAPS LOCK,
6 CTRL, **7** DELETE (on some typewriters)

Task 3
SHIFT Produces upper-case characters.
SHIFT LOCK Keeps the shift in operation without having to hold down the shift key.
CAPS LOCK Produces a mixture of upper-case and lower-case characters.

Task 4
```
 2   6  &   6  3   –  =  –
 4   i  I   I  5   ;  +  ;
 6   b  B   B  7   /  ?  /
 8   o  O   O  9   0  0  0
10   1  1   !  1
```

Task 5 Student A
BREAK Resets the computer to its original condition by clearing the program and all data from the main memory.
SPACE BAR Produces a blank space which counts as a character.
CURSOR KEYS Move the cursor to any position on the VDU screen.
Student B
RETURN Enters the characters on the screen into the CPU.
ESCAPE Stops the program without losing the program or data from the main memory.
COPY Allows characters to be copied from one part of the screen to another.

Task 7
50 2 key pressed without shift
60 Space bar not used after INPUT
70 / key pressed with shift
80 T key held down too long
90 Shift lock used instead of caps lock
100 O key pressed instead of 0
110 Typed without caps lock or shift

Task 8
1 because, **2** However, **3** therefore, **4** because

Task 9 Examples
1 When I is pressed with CAPS LOCK, I is produced.
2 When 0 is pressed with or without SHIFT, SHIFT LOCK or CAPS
3 LOCK, 0 is produced.
  When 1 is pressed with SHIFT or
4 SHIFT LOCK, ! is produced.
  When 1 is pressed with CAPS
5 LOCK, 1 is produced.

Task 10
1c **2**a **3**e **4**f **5**b **6**d

Task 11/12 Examples
Extra keys: numeric keypad.
Extra editing keys: HOME, CLEAR, LINE INSERT CHARACTER, LINE DELETE CHARACTER, SCROLL
Extra function keys: HELP, UNDO, REPEAT, CALCULATE, PRINT, INTERRUPT, MENU, FINISH, STOP
Missing keys: BREAK, SHIFT LOCK, COPY, , |.
Different labels: ESC for ESCAPE, CONTROL for CTRL, arrow for RETURN TAB, DELETE.
Different keyboard positions: ESCAPE, arrow keys, DELETE, most symbols, user-defined function keys.

Task 14
1 Thirty space if space S dollar space equals space open quotes end (in capitals) close quotes space then space GOTO space two hundred

2 Twenty-five space let space T space equals space T space plus space open bracket F star two oblique N close bracket
3 Forty space PROC underscore move (in small letters) colon input space open quotes (capital C) Cost of one hundred space at sign space ten p space question mark space close quotes semi-colon space capital C
4 Twenty space if space M percent space greater than space minus one space or space M percent space less than space twelve space then space print space open quotes (capital C) Can't use close quotes
5 Sixty space L-D-A space ampersand ten space backslash MASK space colon stop loop space bit space via space plus thirteen

UNIT FOUR
Task 1
1 When a device is online, it is connected to and controlled by the CPU whereas when it is offline, it is independent of the CPU.
2 A key station is a device which transfers data from keyboard to disc or tape, which enables it to be quickly input to the computer.

Task 2/3
keypunch **8**, numeric keypad **6**, touchpad **10**, mouse **3**, trackerball **7**, joystick **2**, lightpen **1**, graphics tablet **9**, voice recognition device **4**, measuring device **5**

Task 4
1 a numeric keypad, **2** a graphics tablet, **3** a joystick, **4** a mouse or trackerball, **5** a voice recognition device, **6** a lightpen, **7** a touchpad

Task 5/6
1 . . . by pointing the cursor at the required icon and pressing a button on the mouse.
2 . . . by using the reflection of light, ultrasound, or other methods.
3 . . . by touching the pictures or symbols on the pad.
4 . . . by rotating the ball.
5 . . . by reading the data from the holes.
6 . . . by holding the pen against the screen and moving it.

Task 7 Examples
1 A numeric keypad has keys like a calculator which allows numerical data to be input easily.
2 The joystick lever can be moved in any direction causing the cursor to move quickly about the screen.
3 A lightpen is moved across the monitor screen allowing the user to 'draw' on the screen.
4 Voice recognition devices recognise simple spoken

commands allowing disabled people to use computers without touching the controls.
5 The operator uses the keypunch which causes a series of holes to be punched on the card.

Task 8
1d, 2b, 3a, 4c

Task 9
1 MICR, 2 OCR, 3 Bar codes, 4 OMR.

Task 10
2 software, 3 numeric keys, 4 upper-case characters, 5 digital signal, 6 data, 7 primary store, 8 external memory, 9 offline, 10 log in

Task 11 Example
A joystick works by transforming movements of the stick into movements on the VDU screen. The stick can be moved in any direction, allowing the cursor to be moved quickly round the screen.
A trackerball works by transforming movements of the ball into movements of the cursor on the screen. The cursor is pointed at the required icon and the button is pressed which causes the process to be put into operation.

UNIT FIVE
Task 1
1 displaying one colour only
2 a picture element, the very small sections of a VDU screen
3 A high resolution display is a high quality display made up of a large number of small pixels. A low resolution display uses a small number of large pixels and produces a less detailed display.

Task 2
slow *impact* daisywheel, dot-matrix, *non-impact* thermal, ink-jet
fast *impact* line, *non-impact* line, ink-jet, laser

Task 3
1 daisywheel, 2 dot-matrix, 3 ink-jet, 4 laser, 5 impact line.

Task 4
2i, 3a, 4f, 5b, 6c, 7j, 8e, 9h, 10g.

Task 5 Examples
2 A mouse is used to select a process easily from a menu.
3 A lightpen is used for drawing on the screen.
4 A joystick is used to play fast action games.
5 A voice recognition device is used for controlling computers by speech.
6 A high resolution monitor is used to display high-quality graphics.
7 A low resolution monitor is used for displaying text and crude graphics.
8 A daisywheel printer is used to print 'letter quality' text.

9 A laser printer is used for printing text very quickly.
10 A non-impact printer is used to print text silently.

Task 6
1 Store large quantities of documents.
2 Control the operation of machine tools.
3 In the future, for translation and language teaching.

Task 8 Examples
1 A keypad which is sensitive to touch.
2 A device which is used for storing information.
3 A plotter which has a flat bed.
4 A printer which uses laser light.
5 A monitor which can display in many colours.
6 A printer which operates by the impact of the print head on an inked ribbon and paper.
7 A printer which has a print head in the shape of a wheel.
8 A drive which is used for turning discs.
9 A device which recognises human speech.
10 A printer which prints a whole line of type at a time.

Task 9
Printers can also be divided into fast and slow printers. Fast printers usual'/ print a line or even a page at a time, whereas slow printers print a character at a time. Fast printers are normally used with mainframes. On the other hand, slow printers are used with microcomputers. Fast printers are expensive, whereas slow printers are relatively inexpensive. One type of fast printer is the laser printer. The daisywheel printer is an example of a slow printer.

Task 10 Example
Plotters can be divided into drum plotters and flatbed plotters. With drum plotters, the paper is placed over a drum whereas with flatbed plotters it is placed over a bed. In addition, with the former both the drum and the pen movements produce the drawing. In contrast, with the latter only the pen movements produce the drawing. Both plotters produce the drawing in a series of small steps and both are slow.

UNIT SIX
Task 1
A backing store provides more permanent and almost unlimited storage of information.

Task 2/3
2c, 3f, 4e, 5b, 6a, 7i, 8h, 9d, 10g, 11j.

Task 4 Examples
1 is called formatting.
2 is known as a file.
3 is referred to as the address of the file.

4 is called direct or random access.

Task 5 Examples
1/2 Once the disc has been put into the disc drive, the drive spins it at high speed.
3/4 As the read/write head moves across the surface, it magnetically marks tracks and sectors onto the disc.
5/6 After formatting is completed, the user verifies the disc is formatted correctly.
7/8 As the empty sectors pass under the head, a file is written onto them.
9/10 When the head has found the catalogue address of the file, it moves directly to the correct track.

Task 6
Hard discs *material* aluminium, *sizes* 10", 3.5", *tracks* 200, *computer* mainframe, minicomputer, microcomputer
Floppy discs *material* plastic, *sizes* 3", 3.5", 5.25", *tracks* 40, 80, computer, microcomputer

Task 8
Advantages
Hard discs can hold large quantities of information, fast access times, very reliable.
Floppy discs exchangeable, cheap, fairly reliable.
Winchester discs small, reliable, inexpensive, can hold large quantities of information, fast access times.
Disadvantages
Hard discs expensive.
Floppy discs slower access, limited capacity, information can be easily corrupted, only one disc can be used at a time
Winchester discs not exchangeable

Task 9
1c, 2a, 3b

Task 10
1 video disc, 2 magnetic disc, 3 floppy disc, 4 disc pack, 5 non-exchangeable, 6 exchangeable.

Task 11
1b, 2c, 3d, 4f, 5a, 6e.

Task 12 Example
Cassettes have several advantages. They are cheap, light and compact. In addition, formatting is not required. In other word, tracks and sectors are not marked out. However, there are also some disadvantages. They are unreliable. Moreover, access time is very slow. That is, it takes a comparatively long time to locate information on a cassette.

Task 13 Example
Hard discs have several advantages. They are very reliable and have fast access times. Moreover, they can hold large quantities of information. However, they are expensive.

UNIT SEVEN

Task 1
1 central processor and main memory
2 a slice of silicon with thousands of electronic components and circuits engraved on it

Task 2
1 valves
2 transistors
3 integrated circuits
4 microprocessors

Task 3 Student A
1 Controls all other units in the system also decodes program instructions and makes sure they are carried out in the correct sequence
2 Provide short term storage for special tasks.
3 Holds the address of the next instruction to be carried out.
4 Carries data, control signals, and address signals between units of the CPU.

Student B
1 Performs the calculations and data manipulations.
2 Provide short term storage for special tasks.
3 Temporarily holds the data item currently being processed.
4 Sends out regular pulses to each unit to keep them in step.

Task 4
1 processor, 2 main memory, 3 ALU, 4 program counter, 5 accumulator

Task 5 Examples
a The CPU consists of the central processor and the main memory. The central processor is made up of the control unit and the ALU. The main memory can be divided into the RAM section and the ROM section.
b The control unit and the ALU make up the processor. The RAM section and the ROM section constitute the main memory. The central processor and the main memory make up the CPU.

Task 6 Example
A computer system is composed of software and hardware. Software consists of programs and data. Hardware can be divided into the CPU and peripherals.

Task 7
a 001110
b 101010

Task 8

	RAM	ROM
1	yes	no
2	no	yes
3	yes	no
4	yes	yes
5	yes	no
6	no	yes
7	no	yes
8	yes	no

Task 10
a 0, b 1, c digit, d eight, e bits, f 1, g 8

Task 11
1 one colour of display
2 print in two directions, i.e. forwards and backwards
3 sixteen
4 ten times 1 048 576 bytes (i.e. 10 485 760 bytes) of information
5 a microcomputer
6 bi(nary)
7 multi(-user)
8 micro(fiche)

Task 13 Example
The CPU consists of the central processor and the main memory. The control unit and the ALU make up the central processor. The control unit decodes the other units in the system, decodes the program instructions and makes sure they are carried out in the correct sequence. The ALU performs the calculations and data manipulations. The main memory can be divided into the RAM section and the ROM section. The RAM section temporarily holds the user's programs and data. The ROM section permanently stores the basic operating instructions and languages. It is normally programmed by the manufacturer and cannot be changed.

UNIT EIGHT

Task 1
1 To display graphics and allow the user to 'draw' on the screen. It is normally used for Computer Aided Design.
2 By using telecommunications links, e.g. telephone lines.

Task 2
Components 1 keyboard, printer, 2 keyboard, internal processor, VDU screen, 3 keyboard, internal processor, VDU screen, lightpen
Features 1 hardcopy output, 2 own internal processor, 3 used for Computer Aided Design

Task 3 Student A
1 Allows software and hardware to be shared by a large number of users.
2 Provides network over a relatively small area.
3 Converts signals between computers and telephone lines to the correct form.
4 Allows communication of data over very long distances by receiving, amplifying and re-transmitting signals.

Student B
1 Allows software and hardware to be shared by a large number of users.
2 Provides network over a larger area.
3 Allows transmission of data as pulses of light at high speed with very low levels of interference.
4 Transmits data over long distances and over water.

Task 4 Examples
1a Both dedicated lines and dialled lines can be used in Wide Area Networks.
b Unlike dedicated lines, dialled lines are only connected when needed.
2a Both analogue signals and digital signals are used in data communications systems.
b Analogue signals are often used in electrical measuring instruments whereas digital signals are used in computers.
3a Both Local Area Networks and Wide Area Networks are connected by cables.
b Local Area Networks are confined to small areas whereas Wide Area Networks are connected over large areas.
4a Like ordinary telephone cable, fibre optics cable can be used for connecting networks.
b In contrast to ordinary telephone cables, fibre optics cables give very low levels of interference.
5a Both microwave radio links and satellite links are used to transmit high frequency signals over long distances.
b Unlike microwave radio links, satellite links can be used to transmit messages from continent to continent.
6a Both input devices and output devices are known as peripherals.
b Input devices are used for entering data into a computer whereas output devices are used for bringing data out of a computer.
7a Both impact printers and non-impact printers can be connected to a microcomputer.
b Unlike impact printers, non-impact printers are very quiet in operation.
8a Like mainframe computers, microcomputers consist of a CPU, main memory and peripherals.
b In contrast to mainframe computers, micro-computers are reasonably portable.

Task 5
1 telex, 2 fax, 3 electronic mail, 4 teletext, 5 viewdata

Task 6
1 fax, 2 teletext, 3 telex, 4 fax, 5 viewdata, 6 teletext, 7 electronic mail, 8 fax, 9 viewdata

Task 7
1 tele(text), 2 video (disc), 3 data(base), 4 tele(printer), 5 video(tex), 6 tele(communications), 7 tele(type terminal), 8 data (communications system), 9 tele(x)

Task 8 Example
The diagram shows an electronic mail system linking London and New York.
In the USA the system consists

of a VDU and computer which are linked by a modem to telephone lines. The modem converts digital signals from the computer into analogue signals suitable for ordinary telephone wires. These lines then link the system to a dish aerial.

In the UK the system is made up of a VDU and computer connected by a modem to fibre optic cables. These allow information to be sent over distances with very little interference. These cables link with a dish aerial.

The most important component is the communications satellite which receives microwave signals from one dish aerial and re-transmits them to the other.

This system allows messages to be sent easily over very long distances. The computer memory contains a mailbox where messages can be stored. Users can search the mailbox to find messages addressed to them.

Task 9
This diagram shows a multi-user system. It consists of a CPU and a multiplexor which allows the computer to be linked to six terminals. Three of the terminals are linked directly to the multiplexor. The other three are remote access terminals and are linked by telephone lines. Modems are used at both ends of these links.

Unlike the electronic mail system, this system does not link computers. It links a mainframe computer to a number of terminals. Its purpose is to allow a number of users, some at a distance, to use one mainframe computer. Whereas the electronic mail system is designed for sending messages from one user to another, this system allows users access to a computer for a wide range of purposes. Like the electronic mail system, some of its components are linked by telephone lines through the use of modems. However, this system has no satellite links between continents.

UNIT NINE
Task 1
1 Machine code is the only language understood directly by a computer.
2 A computer language in which each instruction translates into many machine code instructions.

Task 2
High-level languages *advantages* resemble English, easier to write, modify and understand, *disadvantages* use up more memory, slow down execution of program
Low-level languages *advantages* operate at high speed, use minimum of memory,

disadvantages very difficult for humans to use, takes a very long time to write programs, complex

Task 3
Only key words have been noted – pronouns, prepositions, helping verbs have been omitted. Only main points are noted – the definitions of interactive and the example of user-friendly have been omitted. The problems caused by the many dialects of basic have been summarised by 'but many dialects exist'. These are ways of reducing a text to its essentials for easier reference or memorising.

Task 5
1 BASIC or LOGO, 2 FORTRAN, 3 ALGOL, 4 BASIC, 5 PASCAL, 6 BASIC or LOGO, 7 COBOL or ALGOL, 8 BASIC or LOGO, 9 FORTRAN, 10 PASCAL, 11 LOGO, 12 LISP

Task 6
1d, 2e, 3b, 4c, 5a
1 Even though Basic is found on most microcomputers, there are many different dialects.
2 Although PASCAL has a very clear structure, it is more difficult to learn than BASIC.
3 Although high-level languages can be understood by humans, they cannot be understood directly by computers.
4 Machine code can be processed very quickly even though it is difficult to read and write.
5 FORTRAN is widely used in engineering although it is one of the oldest computer languages.

Task 7
When a high-level program is input and run, compiling causes the complete program to be translated into machine code program. The compiled machine code program then has to be run in order to output the results. Interpreting, on the other hand, causes the high-level program to be translated into machine code, one line at a time, to output the results.

Task 9
Compiling *advantages* high-level program only has to be translated once, program can be executed very quickly, *disadvantages* uses a lot of memory
Interpreting *advantages* allows programs to be interactive, makes writing and debugging programs easier, helpful error messages are displayed when errors occur, does not use a huge amount of memory, *disadvantages* slows down the execution of programs

Task 10
1 American Standard Code for Information Interchange
2 LISt Processing
3 Random Access Memory

4 Beginners All-purpose Symbolic Instruction Code
5 BInary digiT
6 PICTure ELEment
7 FORmula TRANslator
8 Programmable Read Only Memory
9 Common Business Oriented Language
10 Computer Aided Design

Task 12 Example
First, the number of nights is keyed in. If the number of nights is less than or equal to 2, the rate is 20, If the number of nights is not less than or equal to 2 but is less than or equal to 6, the rate is 18. If the number of nights is not less than or equal to 6, the rate is 15. The bill is calculated by multiplying the number of nights by the rate. If there are other charges, these are added to the bill. Finally, the bill is printed out.

UNIT TEN
Task 1
1 a collection of application programs kept in backing store
2 calculating employees' wages

Task 2
1 data, 2 applications packages, 3 applications packages, 4 database programs, 5 word processor programs

Task 3 Example
Operating systems *main function* manage and co-ordinate all hardware and software, provide communications between computer and user; *examples of functions* control disc drive, display prompts, keep log of terminals used.
Utility programs *function* perform simple tasks; *examples* housekeeping routines – copying files from tape to disc, merging files, performing screen dumps.
Language translators *function* translate programs in computer languages into machine codes; *examples* giving error messages, displaying listings of programs on VDU
Database management systems *function* allows data from a database to be used by different applications programs

Task 4
1 operating system, 2 utility, 3 assembler or interpreter or compiler.

Task 5
1e, 2d, 3b, 4f, 5a, 6c

Task 6
1 Applications programs are designed for general use so that thay can be used in many different situations.
2 Custom programs are specially written by the user to suit a particular situation.
3 A program library is often kept in backing store to provide easy

access to a range of programs.
4 A word processor justifies each line of text so that they will form a straight line.
5 A high resolution monitor is used to display detailed graphics.
6 A graphics terminal includes a lightpen so that the user can 'draw' on the screen.

Task 8
processing manager in overall charge, co-ordinates the work of others
applications programmer writes and modifies applications programs, may use high-level languages
data preparation supervisor controls the data preparation department
data control clerk checks data handed in to the data preparation department and returns it to the user when the job is complete
systems analyst studies existing systems and advises whether they can be computerised, designs new computerised systems and puts them into operation
systems programmer writes and modifies systems programs, works with low-level languages
computer operator controls and maintains hardware, runs programs and monitors progress of each job
file librarian looks after files, keeps them up to date

Task 10
The job of programmers is to write and modify computer programs. If they are Systems Programmers, they will be involved with systems programs such as operating systems, utilities and language translators. They will then use low-level computer languages such as assembly language or machine code.
   If they are Applications Programmers, they will be involved with applications programs such as payroll programs, database programs, wordprocessor programs and spreadsheet programs. They may, perhaps, use some high-level language such as FORTRAN, ALGOL, COBOL or LISP. In a large computer department, the programmers, under the supervision of the Chief Programmer, will produce the programs required by a Systems Analyst.

UNIT ELEVEN
Task 1
microcomputer with QWERTY keyboard and integral numeric keypad, mouse, monitor, NLQ dot matrix printer, daisywheel printer, dual disc drive, or Winchester, modem.

Task 2 Student A
1 database

2 database
3 diary planner
4 graphics
Student B
1 database
2 drug interaction
3 mail merging
4 accounts package

Task 3
1 database, 2 database and drug interaction, 3 diary planner, 4 mail merging, 5 graphics, 6 accounts package

Task 4
2 A database would be used to find files quickly.
3 An accounts package would be used to ensure the accounts are accurate.
4 A graphics program would be used to compare sales from year to year.
5 A database would be used to keep a record of all customers.
6 A graphics program would be used to produce diagrams for company documents.
7 A spreadsheet would be used to keep a record of stock.
8 A spreadsheet would be used to calculate tax on the price of goods.

Task 5
1 a category of information
2 the field which is unique to the record. It is used for ordering the records.

Task 6
See **Task 8**

Task 7
1 edit, 2 search, 3 wildcard, 4 creating, 5 sorted, 6 key field, 7 fields, 8 deleted, 9 updated, 10 merged

Task 8 Example
The only advantage of a manual filing system is that it is cheap to set up. However, it has many disadvantages when compared to a computer database. For example, it is expensive to run and needs a lot of space. In addition, files have to be stored in one order. Furthermore, records can be mislaid and need updating and other changes mean rewriting the file.
   In contrast, a computer database is cheap to run although it is expensive to set up. It allows records to be sorted and searched quickly and automatically. Complex searches for more than one field and for general information can be made. In addition, by using wildcard characters, searches for incomplete information can be made. Records cannot be lost easily although breakdowns can occasionally occur. A major advantage is that large amounts of information can be stored in a small space. One disadvantage is that security of information has to be ensured so

that unauthorised people cannot have access to the files.

UNIT TWELVE
Task 1
1 in backing store, or on ROM chips
2 a list of choices displayed on the VDU screen

Task 2 Student A
1 **Word-wrap** automatically moves a word to the beginning of a new line when there is not enough space left on a line for the next complete word.
2 **Embedded codes** are instructions which control how the text is printed out, e.g. with underlining.
3 **Justification** makes the edges of the text straight.
Student B
1 **Editing facilities** are features which allow the text to be changed, e.g. by deleting, adding or moving text.
2 **A spelling checker** identifies any incorrect or unfamiliar spelling in a text before it is printed.
3 **Mail merging** allows names and addresses from a database to be inserted automatically in standard letters.

Task 3
1 left and right justification, 2 spelling checker, 3 editing facilities, 4 mail merging, 5 embedded codes, 6 word-wrap facility

Task 4
1 When/As, 2 until, 3 when, 4 before, 5 After/Once/When, 6 Before, 7 before, 8 After/Once/When

Task 5
1 to, 2 than, 3 be, 4 of, 5 Because, 6 in, 7 can, 8 which, 9 therefore/hence/ thus, 10 of

Task 6
1 by, 2 for, 3 into, 4 with, 5 for, 6 at, 7 from, 8 to

Task 7
1 A business person
2 Column C is the result of multiplying column A by column B.
3 100
4 total cost

Task 9
2 A4 * B4, 3 D2 − C2 * B2/100, 4 E2 + E3 + E4.

Task 10
1 high-level languages, 2 printers, 3 data communications services, 4 hardware, 5 storage devices, 6 language translators

Task 11 Examples
1 systems analyst, applications programmer, data controller, file librarian

2 systems program, applications program, data
3 teletype terminal, VDU terminal, graphics terminal
4 trackerball, mouse, VDU, lightpen, graphics tablet
5 network, stand-alone, multi-user

Task 12 Example

A word processor and a typewriter are both used for producing texts. Both have QWERTY keyboards. However, the word processor has many advantages. The main advantages are that texts can be changed and edited easily. For example, letters and words can be deleted or added, and sections of text can be moved without having to retype the entire text. In addition, the layout and printout can be varied. Another advantage is offered by the word-wrap facility which automatically moves a word onto a new line when there is not enough space for it on the line being typed. Word processors will also store texts which can be used again and again or changed as the user wishes. In addition, by using a mail merging program standard letters can be personally addressed to a large mailing list.

Computer Quiz Answers

Unit 1
1 mainframe
2 micros
3 program
4 Central Processing Unit
5 peripherals
6 Visual Display Unit
7 keyboard
8 storage
9 main memory
10 network

Unit 2
1 prompt
2 cursor
3 return
4 password
5 BASIC
6 log
7 LOAD
8 RUN
9 LIST
10 SAVE

Unit 3
1 QWERTY
2 characters
3 autorepeating
4 caps lock
5 escape
6 hash
7 ampersand
8 apostrophe
9 backslash
10 asterisk

Unit 4
1 offline
2 keypunch
3 numeric keypad
4 mouse
5 joystick
6 lightpen
7 Computer Aided Design
8 graphics tablet
9 Optical Character Recognition
10 bar codes

Unit 9
1 machine code
2 Assembly language
3 assembler
4 interactive
5 highlevel language
6 FORTRAN
7 Common Business Oriented Language
8 flowchart
9 interpreter
10 compiler

Unit 10
1 software
2 custom programs
3 database program
4 spreadsheet program
5 integrated package
6 systems programs
7 operating system
8 Database Management System
9 systems analyst
10 data processing manager

Unit 11
1 dotmatrix printer
2 daisywheel printer
3 graphics program
4 update
5 database
6 file
7 field
8 key field
9 wildcard characters
10 merge

Unit 12
1 word processing program
2 What You See Is What You Get
3 wordwrap
4 embedded codes
5 spelling checker
6 justification
7 mail merging
8 spreadsheet program
9 cells
10 scrolling

Unit 5
1 monochrome monitor
2 pixels
3 high resolution display
4 hardcopy printout
5 daisywheel printer
6 dotmatrix printer
7 Near Letter Quality
8 Computer Output on Microfilm
9 Digital to Analogue Converter
10 plotter

Unit 6
1 file
2 access time
3 tracks
4 sectors
5 disc drive
6 format
7 catalogue
8 disc pack
9 Winchester
10 floppy discs

Unit 7
1 central processor
2 Arithmetic and Logic Unit
3 accumulator
4 clock
5 cells
6 Random Access Memory
7 Read Only Memory
8 bit
9 ASCII
10 byte

Unit 8
1 teletype terminal
2 Local Area Network
3 modem
4 acoustic coupler
5 fibre optics cable
6 baud
7 telex
8 teletext
9 viewdata
10 downloading